COFFEE, CAFÉS AND CONVERSATIONS

The Story of the Caffeine Movement

PURVI GANDHI

BOOK COACH & EDITOR

R SRIDHAR

Clever Fox® PUBLISHING

Chennai • Bangalore

CLEVER FOX PUBLISHING
Chennai, India

Published by CLEVER FOX PUBLISHING 2026

ISBN: 978-93-7500-992-4

DISCLAIMER

This book is a work of narrative non-fiction based on research, observation, personal reflection, and publicly available sources. While every effort has been made to ensure accuracy, the author does not claim the material to be exhaustive or definitive.

The views expressed are those of the author and are intended to explore cultural, historical, and experiential aspects of coffee. They should not be interpreted as professional, commercial, legal, or scientific advice.

Any references to individuals, organisations, brands, or establishments are made for illustrative and contextual purposes only. No affiliation, endorsement, or sponsorship is implied.

The author acknowledges the influence of various articles, interviews, and publications in shaping perspectives within this book. These sources are listed in the bibliography for transparency and further reading.

CONTENTS

ACKNOWLEDGEMENTS

With the strength of Lord Shiva and unwavering faith in Yamunaji, I am humbled and grateful to share this dream with you. Every page of this book carries divine grace. Thank you, God, for guiding me, protecting me, and blessing me far beyond what I deserve.

To my parents — thank you for investing in my education and shaping me into the person I am today. Your values, discipline, love, and constant encouragement have been my strongest foundation. Everything I have achieved stands on the shoulders of your sacrifices.

To my husband, Amar — your love, steadfast support, and quiet strength have turned this dream into reality. Thank you for believing in me and for standing beside me through every idea, every experiment, and every late-night brew. I truly feel blessed by God and wonderfully spoilt by you. This book is as much yours as it is mine.

To my coffee buddy and loving son, Nihar — thank you for tasting every brew, listening to every coffee story, and cheering me on with the biggest smile. I love that you have inherited my love for coffee. Sharing this passion with you has been one of my greatest joys.

And finally, to every reader holding this book — thank you for being part of my journey. May every cup of coffee you sip remind you of warmth, connection, and the simple magic that this amazing beverage brings into our lives.

– Purvi Gandhi

It has been a privilege to work closely with Purvi in bringing her long-held vision for this book to life. The depth of her reflections on coffee, and the sincerity of her perspective, made the process both meaningful and inspiring.

I am deeply grateful for the trust and openness that shaped our collaboration, and I hope readers discover in these pages the same thoughtfulness and insight that I experienced throughout this journey.

– R Sridhar

FOREWORD

There are some people who drink coffee.

And then there are people who live it.

When I first encountered Purvi Gandhi — who many affectionately know as Pooh — what struck me was not merely her knowledge about coffee, but her relationship with it. For her, coffee is not a beverage. It is memory, conversation, curiosity, and connection. It is culture in a cup.

In the years that I have spent building spaces like Sante Spa & Cuisines, I have come to understand that food and beverage are never just about taste. They are about experience. They are about how people gather, how ideas are exchanged, and how communities are quietly formed over shared tables. Coffee, perhaps more than anything else, has this remarkable power to bring people together. It slows time just enough for a conversation to deepen. It creates ritual in the midst of chaos.

India's café culture has evolved dramatically over the past two decades. What was once an occasional indulgence has now become an integral part of urban identity. Cafés are offices, confessionals, creative studios, and meeting grounds. Coffee has become a language — one that transcends age and background.

Purvi has observed this transformation not from a distance, but from within it. Through her journey and her vibrant community, she has documented how coffee has shaped lifestyles, friendships, and even aspirations. Her passion spans decades, and yet it retains the freshness of someone discovering her first cup. That is rare.

What makes this book special is not just its subject, but its sincerity. It is not written as an industry manual or a technical guide. It is written as a lived experience. Purvi writes as someone who has wandered into countless cafés with curiosity, who has tasted different brews with openness, and who has understood that behind every cup lies a story — of farmers, baristas, entrepreneurs, and dreamers.

At a time when consumption is often hurried and distracted, this book invites us to pause, notice, appreciate, and understand that something as simple as coffee can be a doorway to mindfulness, creativity, and community.

I believe readers — whether seasoned coffee aficionados or casual café-goers — will find themselves reflected in these pages. You may recognise your own rituals, your own favourite corner table, and your own long conversations that stretched time.

Purvi's voice is warm, unpretentious, and deeply genuine. She does not position herself as an authority looking down from a pedestal, but as a fellow traveller inviting you along. That is perhaps why so many resonate with her. With Pooh.

Books like this matter because they capture cultural moments. They document shifts that we are living through but rarely pause to examine. The coffee and caffeine movement is not merely about trends; it is about how a generation chooses to gather, express, and connect.

It gives me great pleasure to see Purvi bring her decades of passion into a tangible form. This book is a celebration of coffee, cafés, community, and of the simple joy of sharing a cup over a conversation.

I invite you to read it slowly. Preferably with coffee in hand.

Warmly,

AGNELORAJESH ATHAIDE
Founder, Sante Spa & Cuisines | Serial & Social Entrepreneur

SPECIAL NOTE

"Chai pe charcha" has long been a part of our cultural conversations, but today we also find deep connection and meaningful moments over coffee — what I lovingly call "coffee pe connection."

Coffee is more than a beverage; it is a ritual, a pause, a conversation starter, and often a silent companion during moments of reflection and creativity. My own journey with coffee began after my marriage. My mother-in-law, who deeply loved filter coffee, introduced me to the comforting aroma and warmth of this beautiful drink. Over time, coffee became not just a habit but an experience — one that evolved with my own preferences and personal rituals.

Today, my friends often call me "fussy" because I insist on my specific blend — buffalo milk, Bru instant coffee, and the perfect balance of coffee and sugar. But for me, this is not fussiness; it is about honouring personal choice and enjoying what truly resonates. Coffee teaches us that even the smallest details matter, and that taste — much like life — becomes richer when we consciously choose what suits us best.

Purvi Gandhi's book beautifully captures this spirit. Through her passion for coffee, she takes us on an insightful journey — from chai stalls to modern café culture, from instant coffee nostalgia to specialty brews, and from personal identity to global coffee movements. This book is not only about coffee; it is about culture, evolution, community, and the stories that unfold around a cup.

Her exploration of sustainability, economics, and conscious coffee reflects how deeply this beverage has influenced lifestyle, business, and social interaction. It reminds us that coffee is not merely consumed; it is experienced, shared, and lived.

I warmly congratulate Purvi for her dedication and love for coffee, and for creating a guide that informs, inspires, and connects readers to the ever-evolving world of coffee. May this book encourage many to explore their own coffee stories, discover new flavours, and find meaningful connections — one cup at a time.

ROOP LAKHANI
Tarot Coach, Numerologist, Energy Expert, and Consciousness Guide

INTRODUCTION

India is experiencing a quiet but unmistakable coffee revolution. And I have been watching it closely, cup in hand.

For a country long defined by its love for tea, coffee has slowly and confidently found its place as a cultural, social and lifestyle expression. This shift did not happen overnight. It unfolded sip by sip, generation by generation, cup by cup. I like to call this evolving phenomenon The Caffeine Movement.

Before we go any further, let me introduce myself.

I am Purvi Gandhi, but in my coffee world, most people know me as Pooh. I am not a barista, not a roaster, and definitely not an industry insider. I am simply a lifelong coffee lover, an observer, a listener and a storyteller. Through this book, Pooh will be walking alongside you, helping make sense of how coffee quietly found its way into India's everyday life.

My Relationship with Coffee

My affair with coffee began long before the café boom. It goes back to 1991, during my board exams, when a simple cup of coffee helped me stay awake through long study nights. The iconic Nescafé in its red mug became my power-up potion. It was reliable, comforting and energising — exactly what I needed back then.

What started as a practical habit slowly grew into something deeper. Over time, I began noticing how coffee was shaping habits, conversations, workspaces and even identities across the country. The more coffee stories I listened to in cafés, homes, offices and during my travels, the clearer it became that this was not just about taste. It was about experience.

And somewhere along the way, I realised I didn't just like coffee.

I loved it.

When I say love, I mean *lovvveee* coffee. I breathe it. I study it. I research it. I make reels on coffee. My Instagram handle is #CoffeeTalesbyPooh, which should already tell you how serious this relationship is. When the coffee madness truly kicked in, Instagram was my first outlet. I wanted to share what I was discovering with the world.

It wasn't random content. I was reading up on coffee, tracking emerging trends, visiting eclectic cafés, talking to aficionados, roasters and baristas, watching how coffee was brewed, visiting plantations and absorbing everything I could. It felt like a full-blown *junoon*. In fact, when guests came home, I would quietly sneak out, grab a quick coffee at a nearby café, and slip back in. Wink. Wink.

Definitely, something was brewing in the coffee world. Several forces were coming together at the same time. The rise of specialty coffee, innovative brewing techniques, easier access to global coffee knowledge, and the rapid expansion of both homegrown and international coffee chains were transforming coffee from a functional beverage into something sensory, educational and social.

At the time, I had no idea I was part of a much larger cultural shift. I was just trying to stay awake! But that first cup marked the beginning of a lifelong relationship with coffee, one that would eventually mirror India's own evolving relationship with it.

Over the years, coffee stayed with me through workdays, conversations, travels and quiet moments. And somewhere between those cups, Pooh emerged. Observing, curious, and noticing how deeply coffee is woven into our lives.

And tucked away inside all that love was a quiet, hush-hush desire. The desire to author a book on coffee.

How This Book Shaped Up

I wanted Pooh to become a name people automatically associated with coffee. The reading, research, and observing had already been done. Coffee had been living in my head and heart for years. What I didn't have was a clear starting point. I was earnestly looking for someone who could help give shape to this dream. Sometimes, just wanting something deeply is enough to set things in motion.

And that is when the universe decided to step in.

I remember the famous Hindi film dialogue: "If you desire something strongly, the universe conspires to make it happen." The first time I heard that line, I remember thinking, *theek hai yaar, hota hoga*. It sounded nice, but distant.

Today, I can say this with full conviction. That formula works! It really does.

About two months ago, I was at a salon getting a hair wash. Head tilted back, eyes closed, completely relaxed. I was talking on the phone with a friend about how deeply I wanted to move forward with my dream of writing a coffee book, even though I hadn't yet figured out the how.

That is when the lady in the chair next to mine gently leaned over and asked, "Sorry, I overheard you. Did you say you are looking for a book coach and editor?"

I nodded, slightly stunned.

"My name is Payal Talwar," she said. "I know someone experienced who can help you. Would you like to speak to him? His name is R Sridhar."

And just like that, numbers were exchanged. Phone calls were made. Meetings were fixed. Book outlines were discussed. Deadlines were decided.

And here we are! Who said dreams don't become realities?

This Book

While coffee is everywhere today, there are surprisingly few books that talk about India's growing coffee culture in a simple, relatable way. We hear the words — cappuccino, espresso, mocha — but don't really know how to distinguish between them. This book is my attempt to change that. Through personal stories, everyday observations, brewing evolution, café culture and industry insights, I hope to help you understand coffee a little better, and make it feel less intimidating.

Whether you are a casual drinker, a curious explorer, or a devoted enthusiast, this book invites you to pause, sip and look at your cup differently. Because today coffee in India is no longer just a beverage. It has become The Caffeine Movement.

Welcome in.

I am Pooh.

CHAPTER 1

FROM CHAI STALLS TO COFFEE CUPS

This book is about coffee, yes. But before we get comfortable with coffee, we need to talk about its big brother — tea. Especially in India. *Bhai*, chai is after all, *bhaichaara* in our country, isn't it?

If you are one of the tea-vs-coffee *debatewallahs*, then here's some solace for you tea people.

Tea entered our lives long before coffee became popular. In parts of north-eastern India, particularly Assam, wild tea plants had been growing quietly for hundreds of years. It wasn't until the early 19th century that tea truly stepped into the spotlight. That's when the British East India Company began pushing for tea to be cultivated on a large scale.

The reason was simple. Britain loved tea, but it didn't want to rely entirely on China for its supply. So, plantations were set up in India, and before long, large tea estates appeared across Assam and Darjeeling, transforming tea into a booming business.

Indians, of course, didn't drink tea the way the British did. And as is our way, we adapted it. We added the spices already familiar to our kitchens — ginger, cardamom and cloves — and chai was born.

Affordable, quick to prepare and full of flavour, chai slipped effortlessly into Indian life. It showed up in homes, on street corners, at railway stations and in offices. Long before coffee became fashionable, chai had already claimed its place as the nation's everyday comfort drink.

Enter Coffee

Now let's step back a little and look at how coffee first arrived in India. This part always feels special to Pooh.

Coffee was brought into India in the late 17th century by a Sufi saint named Baba Budan. Legend says he smuggled seven coffee beans — *just seven* — from Yemen and planted them in the hills of what we now call Chikmagalur in Karnataka.

Those hills later came to be known as Baba Budan Giri, a quiet tribute to a small but powerful act. From those seven beans grew the roots of India's coffee story! Isn't that incredible?

What followed was very different from tea's journey. Coffee entered India gently and organically, shaped by one man and a handful of seeds.

Tea, on the other hand, arrived later and grew rapidly through colonial scale and structure.

Two beverages. Two beginnings. Two very different paths.

Interesting Folklore

To understand coffee's deeper story, however, we must travel further back.

Wild coffee plants originated in Ethiopia. Folklore speaks of a goat herder named Kaldi who noticed his goats unusually energised after consuming bright red berries. Whether or not the story is literal truth, it captures something essential: coffee's earliest identity was tied to alertness and vitality.

From Ethiopia, coffee travelled to Yemen, where it was first cultivated, roasted and brewed as a beverage. The port of Mocha became synonymous with its trade. By the sixteenth century, coffee had spread across the Arabian Peninsula, into Cairo, Damascus and Istanbul. Debates arose about its permissibility, but its popularity only deepened.

Coffee houses soon became spaces of gathering — places where merchants negotiated, scholars debated and ordinary people conversed. When coffee reached Europe through Mediterranean trade routes, these houses evolved into centres of intellectual exchange. In cities such as London and Amsterdam, coffee houses became arenas of discussion and dissent.

And eventually, Baba Budan and his seven seeds brought that coffee magic into India.

Two beverages. Two journeys.

Tea in India grew through empire and plantation. Coffee grew through trade, ritual and gradual cultivation. Tea became the nation's comfort drink. Coffee would take longer to find its identity.

But its time was coming.

COMING UP NEXT > Coffee's Quiet Beginnings in India

CHAPTER 2

COFFEE'S QUIET BEGINNINGS IN INDIA

This phase traces coffee's gradual journey into India's public life, leading up to the decades between the 1960s and 1980s when coffee was yet to have a national identity.

After Chikmagalur, coffee slowly spread across South India and found a comfortable home. Strong filter coffee — or filter kaapi, as it's lovingly called — became part of everyday life. If you have a South Indian friend, you'll understand this completely. Brewed at home and often blended with chicory, kaapi wasn't something you ordered outside. It was something you grew up with.

South Indians wake up early, and for many, the day simply doesn't begin without a hot, frothy cup of filter kaapi. Walk down a street in Chennai or in one of Tamil Nadu's smaller towns before dawn, and you'll see a scene that feels almost meditative.

A street kaapi vendor, half-awake yet fully focused, pours hot coffee from one container to another, sometimes from a height of nearly two feet, just to get that perfect froth. All this happens as the sky slowly lightens, the streets remain quiet, and the aroma of coffee announces the arrival of a new day.

Nutritionists might raise an eyebrow about the calorie count in filter coffee but ask a Tamilian or a Kannadiga and you are likely to hear the same response — *"Poda! Kaapi comes first, rest can wait!"*

Even the way coffee was consumed felt different. Not in mugs or glasses, but in a tumbler and davara, poured back and forth, cooled gently and sipped slowly. Drinking coffee was never rushed. It was a small ritual, woven into the rhythm of the morning.

(See box: The Tumbler and Davara)

Meanwhile, most of India remained firmly rooted in chai culture. Tea dominated public spaces — offices, railway stations, street corners and homes. Coffee existed, but largely as an occasional indulgence, mostly confined to South India and rarely thought about beyond that.

During this phase, coffee had presence but not reach. It was familiar, but not aspirational. The caffeine movement had begun, but it was still finding its footing.

Enter The Indian Coffee House

Coffee had been grown in India for centuries, but the idea of coffee houses took time to evolve. By the 19th century, coffee houses began appearing in cities like Madras and Calcutta. There was just one catch. These spaces were largely reserved for Europeans. Indians were not welcome, thanks to the racial policies of the British rulers.

However, that didn't sit well for long.

By the late 1890s, the idea of creating Indian-run coffee houses began taking shape. In 1936, the first Coffee Board outlet opened in Churchgate, Bombay — the precursor to what later became Indian Coffee House. It was started by the Coffee Cess Committee and operated by the Indian Coffee Board.

Over the next decade, these coffee houses spread steadily. By the 1940s, there were nearly 50 coffee houses across British India. Coffee was finally stepping out of homes and into shared public spaces.

Then Came a Turning Point

In the mid-1950s, a policy change led the Coffee Board to decide that it would shut down the coffee houses altogether. That could have been the end of the story. But instead, it became the beginning of something much bigger.

Encouraged by communist leader A. K. Gopalan, known fondly as AKG, the workers of the Coffee Board organised themselves and launched a movement. They demanded that the outlets be handed over to them. After sustained effort, the Board agreed.

As a result, the coffee houses were reborn as Indian Coffee House, run by Indian Coffee Workers' Co-operatives.

The first co-operative began in Bangalore in August 1957, followed closely by Delhi later that year. Over time, co-operatives emerged in other cities, and the network grew steadily. Today, there are over a dozen co-operative societies running Indian Coffee Houses across states including Kerala, West Bengal, Karnataka, Madhya Pradesh, Rajasthan, Chandigarh and more.

More Than Just Coffee

What made Indian Coffee House special wasn't just the coffee.

These spaces evolved into something far larger than cafés — they became living rooms of dissent. Students, journalists, doctors, lawyers, bureaucrats and activists gathered here for long conversations. Ideas were debated. Opinions were challenged. Movements were shaped.

If you studied in a university campus during those decades, chances are the Indian Coffee House nearby felt like an extension of your classroom. The outlet at Punjab University, for instance, became legendary among students.

Some accounts suggest that during the Emergency (1975 – 1977), certain outlets were temporarily shut down because they were seen as influential hubs of political discussion and dissent.

Before coffee became trendy, before lattes had foam art and cafés had playlists, coffee in India had already found its voice. It was thoughtful, political and deeply social.

And with that, Phase One gently ends.

The next chapter is Pooh's favourite for it was the era when her love for coffee started brewing. A love that gave her – well, in a way – her life purpose!

The Tumbler and Davara

A tumbler and davara are the traditional vessels used for South Indian filter coffee.

The tumbler is a tall metal cup that holds the hot coffee, usually made of stainless steel to retain heat. The davara is a shallow, wide bowl placed beneath it.

Coffee is poured back and forth between the two to cool it slightly, mix it evenly and create a light froth on top. Simple and practical, this small ritual turns coffee drinking into an unhurried, mindful experience.

COMING UP NEXT > The Instant Era

CHAPTER 3

THE INSTANT ERA

Now this is where things really start getting interesting.

If the first phase of coffee in India was slow, regional and ritual-driven, the second wave came in with speed. Literally. The 1970s and 1980s changed everything, because coffee no longer wanted to wait.

Enter instant coffee. Globally, this mass-market expansion is often described as the First Wave of coffee.

No grinding or brewing, and no filters to wash. Just hot water, one spoon, stir, sip. Done.

Brands like Nescafé and Bru quietly removed effort from coffee-making, and in doing so, they changed Indian homes forever. Coffee stepped out of South Indian kitchens and walked confidently into urban, middle-class households across the country. It became quicker, easier and far more accessible.

And advertising helped, of course. Coffee was no longer just a drink. It became a symbol of energy and movement — a reflection of modern life. Students burning the midnight oil. Professionals racing deadlines. Families embracing a more urban rhythm. Coffee looked young and ambitious.

Innovative packaging also helped. From bottles to pouches to sachets, coffee became instant in many ways.

Pooh's fascination with coffee began during this period.

Two Types of Instant Coffee

When it comes to instant coffee, there are two main ways it is brewed. Most of us don't think about this while stirring our cup, but the process makes a big difference to flavour, quality and cost.

The first is freeze-dried instant coffee. In this method, brewed coffee is frozen and then the ice is removed gently. Since the process is slow and careful, more of the original coffee flavour is retained. The result is a better-tasting cup, but the method is expensive and complex. That is why freeze-dried coffee is usually positioned as premium and delivers higher margins, even though it is not used as widely.

The second is spray-dried instant coffee. Here, brewed coffee is sprayed into a hot chamber, where the water evaporates almost instantly, leaving behind coffee granules. This method is much faster and cheaper, which makes it ideal for mass production. However, much of the flavour is lost in the process. Spray-dried coffee is widely used and more affordable, but it operates on lower margins.

One prioritises flavour; the other prioritises scale. And now you know why not all instant coffees taste the same.

Nescafé vs Bru

This phase also gave us one of India's most enduring brand rivalries. And honestly, every good story needs one.

Let's Start With Nescafé

Nescafé's story began much earlier, in the 1930s, when the Brazilian government approached Nestlé, the Swiss behemoth, with a problem. They had a massive surplus of beans and no easy way to preserve them. Nestlé stepped in, and Max Morgenthaler led a long research project to solve this issue.

Seven years later, in 1938, the solution arrived in the form of a soluble coffee powder that retained flavour and dissolved instantly in hot water. They called it Nescafé. "Nes" derived from Nestlé and "café" from coffee. Nestle's coffee.

The technology behind it was fascinating. Concentrated coffee was sprayed as a fine mist into a heated tower, where the droplets turned into powder almost instantly. For the first time, coffee could be made without brewing.

And the world loved it.

During World War II, Nescafé became a staple for American soldiers. Instant coffee had already gained momentum during World War I, when inventor George C. L. Washington scaled up production for the military. Soldiers fondly called it "a cup of George".

A soldier writing from the battlefields of World War I in 1918 described how, despite the harsh conditions — the mud, rain, constant gunfire and chaos around him — a simple cup of instant coffee brought a moment of comfort and normalcy. He noted that it took only a minute to heat water and prepare the coffee, offering a small but meaningful relief amid the turmoil of war.

By World War II, instant coffee was everywhere. G.I.s called it "a cuppa Joe". The U.S. Army ordered massive quantities of coffee for troops, even rationing civilian supply to prioritise soldiers. After the war, brands like Nescafé and Maxwell House heavily advertised instant coffee to veterans and their families. Convenience had won hearts.

It took another 25 years for Nescafé to come to India. When it did, in 1963, India wasn't really a coffee-drinking nation. Coffee still carried the idea of effort — something that took time and attention.

Nescafé shattered that belief.

"The coffee with life in it. Made in just 5 seconds."

That advertising slogan changed everything.

And oh, the red mug. That iconic red mug became a symbol of energy, alertness and modern living. In India, Nescafé clearly knew who it was talking to. Urban youth. Early mornings. Busy lives. Aspirations.

"*Ho shuru har din aise, ho shuru har pal aise.*"

Pa PaRaPa Pa Ra Ra.

If you lived through that era, that tune is probably playing in your head right now.

Pooh remembers that red mug and those ads kept her awake during her board exams. Nescafé was her study buddy, her comfort and energy boost. This brand didn't just sell coffee; it created a habit.

But Nescafé didn't have the stage all to itself.

Enter Bru

Introduced in 1968 by Brooke Bond, a company best known for tea, Bru did something very smart. It didn't try to compete by being global. It competed by being familiar. Bru introduced India's first coffee-chicory instant blend, something that felt close to the taste of South Indian filter coffee.

The man often credited with bringing instant coffee into Indian homes was T. S. Nagarajan, the former managing director of Brooke Bond. Through the 1980s, even as smaller brands like Indodan tried to enter the space, the real battle remained between Nescafé and Bru.

Nescafé led the instant coffee category. Bru, with its coffee-chicory blends, dominated overall consumption.

In 1984, the rivalry sharpened further when Unilever acquired Brooke Bond. In India, Brooke Bond became part of Hindustan Unilever. Just as it had done in tea, HUL consolidated its coffee brands like Dilkush, Deluxe Green Label, Café and Café Gold under the master brand Bru.

It also introduced regional variants like Bru Malabar, a 90:10 coffee-chicory mix that resonated strongly in the South. By the mid-2010s, Bru had significantly narrowed the gap with Nescafé in instant coffee.

Bru's biggest strength lay in South India, especially Tamil Nadu, where filter coffee culture was already deeply entrenched. As coffee culture spread northwards and café culture grew, Nescafé's global reach helped it hold ground.

Over time, both brands benefited from a deeper shift. Coffee consumption, which had grown at barely two per cent annually until 2000, more than doubled after that. Both Nescafé and Bru expanded across price points, formats and audiences.

Today, both brands command significant shares of India's coffee market.

Why This Phase Really Matters

Beyond brands and market share, this phase did something far more important.

For the first time, many Indians formed a regular relationship with coffee.

Coffee moved from being regional to national, from occasional to everyday, and from ritual to routine. It became associated with ambition, productivity and modern living.

This was the moment coffee stopped being just something you had occasionally and started becoming something you reached for every day.

The caffeine movement had picked up speed. This is the phase where coffee quietly walked into our lives and decided to stay.

DID YOU KNOW?

Globally, it is estimated that two billion cups of coffee are consumed daily and thus it remains one of the most widely traded agricultural commodities in the world.

COMING UP > The Arrival of the Café Culture

CHAPTER 4

THE ARRIVAL OF THE CAFÉ CULTURE

It must have been the late 1990s. Pooh was a student at Mithibai College in Mumbai. Life revolved around lectures, attendance anxieties, group projects, friendships, crushes and, of course, food. Like most college students, she spent a fair amount of time at the college canteen. Not because the food was exceptional, but because that was where life unfolded.

In one quiet corner of the canteen stood a coffee machine.

For ten rupees, you got a cup of machine coffee. Nothing fancy. No latte art or exotic beans. But it was hot, comforting and delivered a much-needed jolt between lectures. At home, Nescafé powered long study nights. Outside, this machine coffee became Pooh's steady companion.

At that stage, coffee was purely functional.

It helped you stay awake and get through the day. You didn't think beyond that.

Graduation followed. Then post-graduation. Marriage too. But the coffee experience barely changed.

Then came a visit to Singapore.

That was when Pooh was introduced to café culture. Cafés as spaces, not just beverage counters. Places where people sat, lingered, talked, worked and paused. She remembers thinking, "How I wish we had this café culture in India."

It seems someone was listening.

One day, her husband casually mentioned, "Have you heard of this new café that's opened in Santacruz? It's called Café Coffee Day." This was around 2000, just a few years after the first CCD had opened in Bengaluru in 1996.

A café? In Mumbai?

Pooh could hardly believe it. "Of course, let's check it out," she said, already excited.

What they walked into felt different.

The CCD Experience

Café Coffee Day, or CCD as it soon became known, neither felt like a restaurant nor like a college canteen. And it certainly didn't feel like home either.

It felt like something in between.

There were proper chairs and tables. Soft music played in the background. The menu spoke of cappuccinos and lattes. Snacks were meant for sharing. Most importantly, there was no pressure to leave.

For her, it was a revelation.

CCD became the place for everything — long conversations, short catchups, group gossip and private heart-to-hearts. Study sessions with very little studying. First dates. Break-up discussions. Quiet time with a book. Sometimes, just sitting alone with a cup of coffee and one's own thoughts.

For Pooh and her husband, cafés soon became preferable to almost anywhere else. If there was time to spare, it was most likely spent at a café.

As café culture began picking up across Mumbai, Pooh had a friend with whom she would venture out almost daily to explore new spots around Khar and Bandra. "Where will you find Pooh?" someone would ask. "Oh, in some café in the vicinity," came the predictable reply. It wasn't entirely a joke. It was a lifestyle.

Around this time, Pooh became acquainted with a fellow coffee lover who she met at Barista. A friendship that began over coffee all those years ago blossomed beautifully. Today, they are best friends in the truest sense. What started as casual coffee outings evolved into something deeper — brews with besties becoming not just a phrase, but a lived reality.

Then came Wi-Fi and charging points, making it even harder to leave. Cafés were no longer just meeting places; they became extensions of home and office.

Cold coffee with whipped cream became Pooh's staple order. At around ₹250, it felt indulgent then. But this ritual brought her immense joy.

On many occasions, sneaking out late evening for a cappuccino with her best friend became routine — a small rebellion wrapped in froth and warmth. Her child's tuition at 6 pm? No problem. Pooh would step out at 5.30, detour to a nearby CCD, and savour a calm cup of coffee before the evening rush resumed.

Coffee was no longer just consumed. It was about the experience. What CCD did exceptionally well was create a space that demanded nothing from you. You didn't have to dress up or order a full meal. You didn't have to rush: you could just be.

For a generation of young Indians, that mattered.

By offering espresso-based drinks at prices that didn't feel intimidating, CCD made coffee trendy without making it inaccessible. It introduced an entire generation to café culture that felt global and modern, yet distinctly Indian.

And then there was that line.

A lot can happen over coffee.

That tagline did more work than most campaigns.

V. G. Siddhartha: The Mind Behind the Movement

CCD was the brainchild of V. G. Siddhartha, an entrepreneur from the coffee estates of Chikmagalur in Karnataka. His family had been growing and exporting coffee for over 130 years. Indian coffee travelled the world, but Siddhartha noticed something missing. Indians themselves weren't really drinking it.

His idea was simple and bold. If Indian coffee could fill cups abroad, why couldn't it be experienced at home?

In 1996, he opened the first Café Coffee Day on Brigade Road in Bengaluru. At a time when tea dominated and cafés were rare, the idea felt radical. The café offered good coffee, a relaxed atmosphere and even a cyber café, a novelty in early internet days. The response was immediate. People came, stayed, and returned.

CCD normalised meeting over coffee instead of chai for a generation of urban Indians. It created spaces where people could talk, work, think or simply pass time. It filled the gap between roadside stalls and expensive restaurants, offering what many later called affordable luxury.

Despite his background in finance, Siddhartha had a sharp instinct for branding and customer behaviour. As noted in the book *Coffee King* by Rukmini Rao and Prosenjit Datta, he often visited cafés incognito, observing customers and returning with ideas. His brief was clear but demanding: make CCD democratic without being downmarket. Comfortable enough for chappals, yet aspirational enough for coffee lovers.

For many years, CCD struck that balance. It turned coffee from a beverage into a habit, a hangout and eventually, a lifestyle.

Enter Barista and the Third Place

Soon after CCD came Barista. Suddenly, CCD had company.

Launched in 2000, Barista brought a more international café aesthetic to India. Espresso machines, lattes, cappuccinos and mochas took centre stage. Coffee was no longer just consumed; it was experienced.

Together, CCD and Barista made coffee social.

They introduced the idea of the third place — neither home nor work — neutral, comfortable spaces where people could meet, relax or simply exist for a while.

People began saying, "Let's catch up for coffee." It no longer sounded odd or pretentious. It sounded normal. The shift was subtle, but significant.

Their success paved the way for newer players like Di Bella and Costa Coffee. In Mumbai, neighbourhoods such as Bandra, Khar, Colaba and Juhu saw small cafés spring up everywhere. Places where conversations flowed easily and time slowed down, just a little.

For Pooh, cafés became her natural habitat.

The Legacy

Whatever followed, one thing is undeniable.

CCD, along with Barista and others, changed India's relationship with coffee. It introduced café culture to a generation. It made coffee aspirational without being intimidating. It created spaces where people gathered, worked, argued, laughed, cried, paused and grew.

For many, including Pooh, cafes were where coffee stopped being just a drink and became a ritual. A small but meaningful part of everyday life.

The timing was not accidental. India's post-liberalisation economy was expanding. Disposable incomes were rising, malls were emerging, and a young urban population was looking for spaces beyond home and office. Café culture arrived exactly when India was ready for it.

Yet Pooh remained curious.

She was waiting for the queen she had encountered during her trips to the US — the Green Lady, Starbucks.

A brand that wasn't just coffee, but aspiration itself.

She had read about Starbucks coming to India. The question was when.

But she didn't have to wait long. Starbucks announced its arrival and transformed the scene completely.

The café culture wave had arrived. But the story of coffee in India was far from done.

DID YOU KNOW?

During internal workshops, V. G. Siddhartha discovered that CCD employees viewed the brand differently. Some saw it as a coffee company, others as a café experience. He clarified that CCD was a café business, not just about coffee. This reportedly influenced a shift in branding, including replacing the coffee leaf in the logo with a dialogue box symbolising conversation and a brand meant to grow beyond coffee and India

COMING UP > Entry of the Green Lady

CHAPTER 5

ENTRY OF THE GREEN LADY

October 19, 2012, was no ordinary day in Pooh's life. She had barely slept the night before. After all, the Green Lady was arriving.

The next evening, she, her husband along with her friends headed excitedly to the Fort area in South Mumbai to visit a newly opened café.

This was not just another café opening. This was Starbucks!

The global brand, led by Howard Schultz, was already familiar to Pooh from her travels abroad, especially in the United States. In New York, sipping an extra-large chocolate mocha iced coffee while walking towards downtown Manhattan had become a quiet ritual. Starbucks was not merely about coffee. It stood for routine, comfort and a sense of belonging.

And now, that very Starbucks was opening in Mumbai.

When they reached Starbucks, the scale of the moment became clear. The road leading to the café was packed. A long queue curved around the entrance. This was no understated launch. It felt like a major event.

Even a glimpse of the logo was enough to trigger excitement. The Starbucks logo features a twin-tailed siren from Greek mythology, chosen to reflect the allure of coffee and the brand's maritime roots in Seattle's port-city heritage.

After nearly an hour of waiting, they finally took their seats inside. The café felt plush and welcoming. It did not try too hard to impress; it felt confident, polished and global.

Backed by its partnership with the Tata Group and branded as Tata Starbucks, the company arrived with immediate credibility. Free Wi-Fi, still a novelty in 2012, drew students, professionals and first-time visitors. The menu struck a careful balance. Cappuccinos and Frappuccinos sat alongside India-specific offerings such as chocolate muffins, croissants, puffs, almond cookies, and sandwiches. Conversations began even before the first sip.

The stores blended local design elements with the global Starbucks aesthetic, creating familiarity without dilution.

Expansion followed quickly. Starbucks outlets appeared across Mumbai, from the Taj Mahal Palace to Oberoi Mall. Celebrities carrying the now-iconic white cups amplified the shift. Coffee became a symbol of aspiration, style, and global identity.

Behind the scenes, technology quietly strengthened the experience. Data helped Starbucks understand customer habits, from ordering times to preferences and frequency of visits. The app enabled personalised offers, saved favourite drinks and improved inventory and staffing through AI-led insights. The technology rarely felt intrusive. Most customers simply experienced it as ease.

Starbucks chose not to compete on price. It competed on experience. While others chased speed and affordability, Starbucks focused on consistency, customisation and atmosphere. Loyalty programmes, digital ease and dependable quality helped it stand out in a crowded market.

The Starbucks Story

The Starbucks experience as we know it almost did not happen.

In 1983, Howard Schultz, then a marketing executive at a small Seattle-based coffee bean roaster called Starbucks, travelled to Milan. He was struck by the espresso bars there. Baristas prepared coffee while engaging with customers, and cafés functioned as social spaces.

Back in Seattle, Schultz persuaded the owners to let him experiment.

"The Italians had created the theatre, romance, art and magic of experiencing espresso," he later said. "I was overwhelmed with a gut instinct that this is what we should be doing."

By 1987, Schultz had acquired the company and began scaling the concept. What began as a small Seattle roaster scaled relentlessly. By 2020, Starbucks operated over 30,000 stores worldwide. By late 2025, that number crossed 40,000. In India alone, Tata Starbucks crossed 500 stores by November 2025, with plans to double the count in the coming years.

Starbucks succeeded not merely by selling coffee, but by reimagining an old habit. It positioned itself as the in-between space — neither home nor office — comfortably bridging both. Coffee once again became a reason to gather, pause and connect — echoing its earliest cultural role centuries ago.

When discussions turn to the second wave of coffee, Starbucks is inevitably mentioned. It did not just sell beverages. It offered choice. Hot or cold. Strong or mild. Espresso, latte, cappuccino, Frappuccino. Beans to take home. Seasonal specials. Menus that adapted to local tastes. Free Wi-Fi that subtly changed how people used cafés.

Pooh noticed that customers did not rush in and out. They stayed, worked, met and conversed.

Pooh noticed something else. Starbucks set a higher standard. "Good enough" was not acceptable. Details mattered. Friendly baristas. Names on cups. Birthday drinks. A complimentary coffee if the wait was too long. These gestures signalled care and intention.

The aim was clear. Starbucks had to feel special, not rushed or careless.

Like any global giant, Starbucks has faced criticism and controversy. Yet it built fierce loyalty, massive scale and a cultural presence that extended far beyond coffee.

By the time you held that green-logo cup, you were not just consuming caffeine. You were part of a narrative.

Where CCD Got It Wrong

For years, Café Coffee Day felt like home to an entire generation. Somewhere along the way, it lost what once made it distinctive.

Between 2012 and 2015, the shift was hard to miss. While newer cafés refreshed their interiors and curated experiences, many CCD outlets remained unchanged — dim lighting, worn furniture, dated ambience. Customer expectations evolved; CCD did not.

As India's coffee palate matured, boutique brands such as Blue Tokai Coffee Roasters and independent neighbourhood cafés introduced artisanal brews and a strong sense of craft. Coffee was no longer just a meeting point — it became an experience. Rapid expansion diluted quality, menus stagnated, service slipped, and CCD struggled to speak to a digital-first audience. It was, in many ways, serving a 2005 customer in a 2020 world.

And that was when Pooh began to wander.

If CCD had once been her comfort zone, exploration now became her ritual. She and her friends started discovering cafés across their neighbourhood — comparing beans, tasting notes, ambience and playlists with equal seriousness.

They found themselves at Coffee By Di Bella for its international flair, at Bombay Coffee House for its old-world charm, at BRU World Cafe for its familiar warmth, at Costa Coffee for its global consistency, and even at Dunkin' Donuts when conversations demanded comfort food alongside caffeine.

Soon, café-hopping became more than socialising — it became research. Pooh developed a reputation for knowing which place had the strongest espresso, the best lighting for pictures, and the quietest corner for long conversations. Whenever her friends debated where to go, she was the café encyclopaedia they consulted.

Going out with her besties in search of the next good brew was no longer occasional — it was a way of life.

When the World Stopped

Things were going smoothly for coffee lovers. Then Covid arrived.

Cafés shut.

Life paused.

The world moved indoors.

But the coffee lover adapted. Confined to home, she began experimenting. New brewing methods. New flavours. New routines.

What emerged was something entirely different.

DID YOU KNOW?

The world's largest Starbucks store is the Starbucks Reserve Roastery in Chicago. Spread across five floors and 35,000 square feet, it roasts coffee on-site. The roaster is the first thing visitors see, celebrating Starbucks' heritage in roasting and coffee craft.

COMING UP > And then, Covid hits

CHAPTER 6

AND THEN, COVID HITS

It was around March 2020. Pooh was getting ready to step out for coffee at her favourite Starbucks. Life had been comfortable. Coffee outings were routine. Instagram was filled with café discoveries. Smaller cafés were being explored, new brews were sampled, and coffee catchups with friends and family had settled into the rhythm of everyday life.

There was talk of a pandemic. India's first case had been reported in Kerala in January but it felt distant and manageable. Something that would pass.

Then, on March 25, the government announced a nationwide lockdown.

The meaning of that word became clear almost immediately. Shops shut. Streets emptied. Offices closed. Life paused. Pooh's café visits ended overnight.

Familiar routines disappeared and daily life shrank to the boundaries of home.

Work moved to dining tables. Conversations shifted to screens. Days blended into one another. Weirdly, the outside world, cafés included, became something discussed cautiously, almost with nostalgia.

For a coffee lover, the absence was sharper than expected. There was no watching baristas prepare an Americano. No quiet corner in a café with a laptop open. No traffic to observe. No background noise to fade into.

Still, the habit did not disappear. Swiggy and Zomato kept delivering to closed doors. Noticing how downcast she was, her husband and son surprised her with a Nespresso coffee machine, ordered on Amazon as her birthday gift. That single, thoughtful gesture lifted her energy and gently shifted her perspective — the lockdown began to feel like an opportunity to try new things rather than something to endure.

Confined indoors, people began experimenting. Baking came first. Sourdough starters, banana bread, and even elaborate meals. Soon, coffee lovers grew restless. They wanted café-style comfort without cafés.

That was when Pooh noticed it.

A drink began appearing everywhere. Instagram reels, WhatsApp forwards, and TikTok videos were whipping them up and making them viral. Hands whisking rapidly. Bowls filling with thick, glossy foam. A spoonful placed carefully over milk.

Dalgona coffee.

Pooh was sceptical. Instant coffee whipped into something indulgent sounded gimmicky. But boredom lowers resistance, and curiosity spreads fast when everyone seems to be doing the same thing.

So, she tried it.

What surprised her was not the taste. It was the process.

Dalgona coffee demanded effort. It did not appear at the push of a button. It required whisking, patience and focus. Watching coffee, sugar and hot water turn into a pale, fluffy foam felt grounding.

At a time when control had slipped away globally, here was something small that responded exactly to effort.

That mattered.

She wrote down the recipe.

Pooh's Dalgona Coffee

Ingredients

- 2 tablespoons instant coffee
- 2 tablespoons sugar
- 2 tablespoons hot water
- 1 cup milk, dairy or plant-based
- Ice cubes, optional

Method

Pooh mixed the coffee, sugar and hot water in a bowl and whipped it, by hand or with an electric mixer, until the mixture turned light brown, fluffy and glossy, forming soft peaks. It took three to five minutes, though time felt oddly flexible during lockdown.

She poured milk into a glass. Hot for comfort. Cold with ice for relief. The whipped coffee was spooned on top. Some stirred it in immediately. Others, Pooh included, preferred to sip through the foam first.

It was simple, indulgent and satisfying.

Soon, Dalgona coffee became a daily ritual. Not because it was extraordinary, but because it broke monotony and added structure to days that otherwise blurred together.

Google Trends rated "Dalgona coffee" as the most searched coffee-related term worldwide during the early months of the pandemic. Searches surged by nearly 1,800 per cent in mid-March 2020; in some regions, interest spiked by over 5,000 per cent within weeks!

The drink took its name from dalgona, a South Korean honeycomb toffee, after actor Jung Il-woo compared the whipped coffee to the candy on a Korean television show in early 2020. The clip went viral. People in quarantine tried it at home and social media did the rest.

As Pooh kept making it, something felt familiar.

In Indian homes, whipped coffee had existed quietly for decades. It was known as *phenti hui* coffee, in which equal parts instant coffee, sugar and hot water were beaten patiently, often by hand, until pale and frothy. The foam was loosened with hot water, topped with milk, and adjusted by instinct rather than measurement.

The difference was not the drink. It was the presentation.

Phenti hui coffee was practical and comforting. Dalgona was more visual and layered. One dissolved into the cup. The other sat on top. One was meant to be consumed. The other was meant to be photographed.

Experts later explained that instant coffee contains melanoidins — the same compounds that create espresso crema — which trap air when whipped with sugar and hot water, forming a stable foam.

Instant coffee, long dismissed as inferior, turned out to be perfectly suited to the moment.

That felt fitting. Pooh remembered her board exam days and her reliance on instant coffee. "I can't believe my poor little instant coffee has found a new cousin," she thought.

In isolation, people were hungry for transformation. Watching basic pantry ingredients turn into something plush felt reassuring. Creating indulgence from what was already available mattered.

Dalgona coffee also fit the social moment. With cafés closed, Instagram needed new material. Latte art and café interiors were replaced by kitchens, bowls and mugs. Dalgona offered participation and visibility.

Coffee shifted from consumption to creation.

Customisation followed. Oat milk. Almond milk. Reduced sugar.

Variations emerged. Matcha Dalgona. Chocolate versions. Spiced whips with cinnamon and caramel.

Eventually, protein-infused and functional versions appeared.

Coffee had come home. For Pooh, this shift felt important. Coffee was no longer only a third-place habit. It became ritual and self-care and a way to mark time when days blurred together. Even those who did not love the taste enjoyed the act of making it.

Years later, long after lockdowns eased, Dalgona coffee did not disappear. Social media mentions continued into 2026. Cafés revisited it. Ready-to-drink versions appeared. What began as a lockdown trend evolved into a flexible base for experimentation.

Its cultural meaning, however, remains tied to that moment.

Dalgona coffee was not just a way to pass time. It was a response to uncertainty. It offered comfort and a sense of control when routines vanished.

For Pooh, it marked a shift. Coffee was no longer something made only by cafés or brands. It became personal, shaped at home, adjusted to taste, and enjoyed in the moment.

When cafés reopened, people returned changed. People returned more curious, less passive, and more aware.

Sometimes, all it takes is a bowl, a whisk and a little patience.

This shift in mindset most likely paved the way for the Third Wave and the rise of specialty coffee.

DID YOU KNOW?

The Indian coffee industry faced an estimated loss of ₹700 crore in the plantation sector in Karnataka alone due to disruptions in harvesting, trading and exports during the 2020 COVID-19 lockdown.

COMING UP > Coffee Brewing at Home

CHAPTER 7

COFFEE BREWING AT HOME

Pooh had not expected brewing coffee at home to become routine so quickly, but it did. What began as trial and error gradually settled into a repeatable process with familiar movements, familiar sounds, and a predictable outcome. Grinding beans, heating water, choosing a method — none of it felt dramatic, yet together it brought a sense of order to the start of the day.

She came to see that home brewing is not a single action but a sequence of small decisions. Alter one variable, whether grind size, water temperature, or brewing time, and the result changes noticeably. Get most of them right and the coffee is reliably good. Get them wrong, and the cup makes that clear.

At its core, brewing coffee at home is an exercise in attention. It does not require specialist equipment or rigid rules, yet it rewards care and repetition. Over time, habits form, preferences sharpen, and the process shifts from something technical to something intuitive.

Getting the Basics Right

Before choosing a brewing method, a few fundamentals apply across the board.

The *ratio of coffee to water* is a useful starting point. Most home brewers operate within a range of 1:15 to 1:18. Stronger ratios produce heavier, more intense cups, while weaker ones can feel thin. Pooh learned that the "right" ratio depends as much on personal taste as on guidelines, and that small adjustments often matter more than sweeping changes.

Water quality plays a larger role than many expect. Since coffee is mostly water, any off flavours show up clearly in the cup. Filtered or clean-tasting water consistently produces better results than hard or heavily treated water.

Temperature matters as well. Water just below boiling, roughly 90–96 °C, extracts flavour efficiently without drawing out excessive bitterness. Pooh did not measure temperature precisely. Instead, she paid attention to balance and adjusted based on taste.

Grinding is another critical step. Whole beans ground just before brewing retain aroma and clarity far better than pre-ground coffee. Using a small digital scale improves consistency, though many home brewers rely on approximation. Different methods call for different grind sizes, but consistency matters more than precision. This didn't apply in Pooh's case because she used to purchase ground coffee beans.

Once these basics become familiar, brewing stops feeling complicated and starts to feel manageable. Pooh often credits her son for patiently mentoring her in the basics of coffee brewing. From pour-over to Moka pot, the language and techniques of coffee slowly became familiar under his guidance.

Pour-over Brewing

This method requires attention, but not complexity.

The setup is simple: a dripper, a paper filter, freshly ground coffee, and hot water. Rinsing the filter removes papery flavours and warms the vessel. The grounds are added next, followed by a small initial pour to allow the coffee to bloom. This brief pause releases trapped gases and prepares the grounds for extraction.

The remaining water is poured gradually, usually in slow spirals, keeping the grounds evenly saturated. The process takes only a few minutes and produces a clean, well-defined cup.

Pour-over coffee highlights acidity and clarity. The flavours are distinct, and the cup feels lighter and more precise. Pooh found this method suited mornings when she wanted structure and a few minutes of quiet focus before the day took over.

French Press

The French press offers a very different experience. Coarsely ground coffee is steeped directly in hot water, without paper filters. After a few minutes, the plunger separates the grounds from the brewed coffee.

The result has a heavier body and more rounded mouthfeel because oils and fine particles remain in the cup. The flavour is less sharp but more substantial.

The French press is simple and tolerant. It does not penalise minor timing errors and works well when you want something comforting rather than precise.

AeroPress

The AeroPress quickly became Pooh's most-used brewer. Compact and efficient, it brews by steeping coffee briefly and then applying gentle pressure to push the liquid through a filter. The process is fast, and clean-up is minimal.

Its defining feature is flexibility. By adjusting grind size, water temperature, brew time, or pressure, the same device can produce a wide range of results, from clean and light to rich and concentrated.

Portable, durable, and forgiving, it suits everyday use. Pooh valued it not for producing exceptional coffee, but for producing consistently good coffee with minimal effort.

Other Common Home Brewing Methods

Several other methods fit easily into home routines.

The Moka pot, used on the stovetop, produces a strong, concentrated coffee that sits between filter coffee and espresso. It pairs well with milk-based drinks.

Cold brew requires the least attention. Coarsely ground coffee is steeped in cold water for several hours, resulting in a smooth, low-acidity concentrate. It rewards planning rather than involvement and works particularly well in warm weather.

Each method responds differently to time, heat, and grind size. Over time, Pooh began choosing methods less by instruction and more by mood, schedule, and context.

Learning Through Repetition

What stood out most to Pooh was that home brewing is not about chasing a perfect cup. It is about familiarity. Over time, the kitchen becomes a place of quiet learning. You notice how different beans behave, how small changes affect taste, and how personal preference shapes judgement.

There is no final technique to master, only habits that settle and improve with use. Brewing coffee at home offers a modest opportunity to slow down, make something with intention, and begin the day on your own terms.

In the end, the best cup is not defined by equipment or method, but by the quiet confidence that comes from making it yourself.

DID YOU KNOW?

Coffee contains over 800 aroma compounds. That is more than wine. These compounds are why fresh coffee has such a rich and layered scent.

COMING UP > Specialty Coffee Takes Over

CHAPTER 8

SPECIALTY COFFEE TAKES OVER

For decades, coffee in India followed a familiar progression.

The first wave was practical. Coffee was mostly instant. It was functional and dependable, consumed to stay awake rather than to be savoured.

The second wave arrived with cafés. Café Coffee Day, followed by international chains such as Starbucks, introduced espresso machines, flavoured drinks and café seating. Coffee became a social activity and a marker of urban aspiration.

After Covid, a quieter shift began. Coffee stopped being just a place or a brand. It became something people noticed.

This marked the beginning of India's specialty coffee movement.

Specialty coffee was not about louder cafés or elaborate menus. It was a change in mindset. People began asking new questions.

Where did this coffee come from?

Who grew it?

How was it processed?

Why did it taste the way it did?

For Pooh, this shift became clear only after she returned to cafés once restrictions eased. She went back not out of habit, but curiosity.

Her first real encounter with this new phase came through Blue Tokai Coffee Roasters.

Before the café experience, however, there was a story that explained why Blue Tokai Coffee Roasters felt different.

Blue Tokai Coffee Roasters

In 2013, long before 'specialty coffee' entered popular vocabulary in India, Namrata Asthana and Matt Chitharanjan were simply looking for a good cup of coffee and could not find one. Instead of settling, they began roasting coffee at home in a small bedroom of Asthana's parents' Delhi apartment.

They bought a modest tabletop roaster and grinder and persuaded a few growers, who typically sold export-quality beans abroad, to sell directly to them. Initially, the coffee was largely for personal use. As Matt would later recall, they assumed there must be others like them. At the time, specialty coffee was effectively unavailable in India.

They were right.

By the end of that year, Blue Tokai Coffee Roasters opened its first roastery and café. A key decision followed. Should they stay small and personal, or scale? They chose to grow, believing that introducing Indians to thoughtfully sourced and carefully roasted coffee was worth the risk. Today, Blue Tokai Coffee Roasters operates over 150 cafés across ten cities, with reported revenues of approximately ₹325 crore in FY25.

When Pooh walked into her first Blue Tokai café, she sensed that origin story immediately.

The space felt intentional and calm. It was not intimidating, just considered. The menu did not overwhelm; it explained. Single origin. Medium roast. Pour-over.

When her cup arrived, it surprised her. The aroma carried a hint of fruit. The first sip was bright, followed by a soft sweetness she could not immediately identify. There was no bitterness or heaviness. The coffee felt clear.

Around her, customers watched their drinks being prepared. Baristas spoke about farms and processing methods conversationally, inviting curiosity rather than instruction.

Blue Tokai was not trying to replace the café culture Pooh already knew. It was reframing it.

Soon after, Pooh visited Third Wave Coffee in Bengaluru.

This experience felt warmer and more familiar, yet equally deliberate. The menu leaned into comfort. Cappuccinos, lattes and cold brews appeared under familiar names, but the beans carried stories. Pooh ordered a latte. It arrived smooth and rounded, with notes of toasted nuts and milk chocolate.

If Blue Tokai asked her to focus on coffee, Third Wave invited her to live with it. This was not competition. It was progression.

Around the same time, Araku Coffee added another dimension. What began as a roastery exporting single-origin beans grown by Indigenous farmers in the Araku Valley to Japan, South Korea and France eventually turned towards Indian consumers. As local demand matured, Araku opened cafés in Bengaluru and later Mumbai, offering earthier, terroir-driven profiles with a strong sense of place.

Then came Subko.

Pooh's first visit left her unsure of what she had walked into. Was it a café, a chocolate bar, a bakery or a design studio? It was all of them.

Founded by Rahul Reddy, Subko took a different approach from the outset. It prioritised craft. The coffee, chocolate, packaging and spaces all felt deliberate. The coffees were expressive and often challenging. Tasting notes read more like wine descriptions than café menus. They demanded attention.

The bean-to-bar chocolate, made from Indian cacao, surprised many with its depth and complexity.

Subko represented the sharper edge of India's specialty coffee movement, where coffee intersected with design, storytelling and a global sensibility. It was not trying to appeal to everyone. It was defining its space.

Specialty coffee in India had grown confident enough to be bold, opinionated and experimental. It no longer felt the need to explain itself.

These cafés were not just serving drinks. They were surfacing stories about growers, regions, harvests, varieties and processing methods, and weaving them into the experience.

This was the third wave of coffee.

It was not about where you sat. Rather, it was about what was in your cup.

Branding shifted from comfort to craft. Beans were labelled by origin. Roasts were described with intent. Farmers were no longer invisible. Traceability and sustainability became part of the value, even if customers did not always articulate it that way.

The transition was not easy. In the early days, growers were sceptical that Indian consumers would not pay for quality coffee without robusta or chicory. Today, many of those same growers are experimenting with fermentation techniques, processing styles and microlots, pursuing flavour profiles that range from delicate florals to layered fruit notes.

Consumers evolved too. Millennials and Gen Z, now the largest specialty coffee-drinking groups, began moving beyond milk-heavy drinks. Baristas became storytellers. They explained not just how to brew, but why a bean behaved the way it did. Customers asked about altitude, processing and tasting notes.

The pandemic accelerated the shift. With cafés closed, home brewing surged. Coffee lovers invested in beans, grinders and equipment, experimenting at home. Retail sales grew as a share of specialty brands' revenue. Once restrictions eased, workshops and cupping sessions became popular weekend activities.

The 'Third Places'

Specialty cafés also evolved into new kinds of third places. They became spaces for community, learning and discovery. Many roasteries now feature tasting bars, manual brewing counters, reading rooms and curated experiences.

India's specialty coffee market is still young, but it is growing fast. Valued at over $3 billion according to TechSki Research, it is expected to more than double in the coming years, driven by rising incomes and increasing consumer curiosity.

For Pooh, this felt like a natural continuation. She had grown up on instant coffee and had lived through café culture. Now she was learning to taste coffee with patience and awareness.

Coffee was no longer about where she sat or which brand she chose. It was about what was in the cup, and why.

Specialty coffee did not replace the earlier waves. It built on them and respected habit while encouraging intention. It gave drinkers vocabulary, choice and agency. India had not stopped loving its cafés. It had learned to listen to its coffee.

For Pooh, this was only the beginning. The journey would take her beyond the cup, into fields and roasteries, into farmers' lives and the science behind every flavour.

DID YOU KNOW?

Lavazza and the Italian Space Agency collaborated to create the ISSpresso, a machine that makes espresso in space.

COMING UP > Sustainability in Every Cup

CHAPTER 9

SUSTAINABILITY IN EVERY CUP

Pooh first sensed that something had shifted when a young girl at the next table abruptly paused her phone call. Holding up a packet of coffee, she asked the barista, "Sorry, can you tell me where these beans are from?"

The barista smiled. "Chikmagalur. Single estate. Washed process."

The girl nodded. "And are they ethically sourced?"

Pooh almost dropped her spoon.

Ten years earlier, the only ethical question around coffee was whether it was strong enough. Now this girl, barely twenty, was asking about sourcing and ethics as casually as one might ask for extra foam.

Pooh stirred her cappuccino and smiled. Something had clearly changed.

When Gen Z Entered the Café

Every generation approaches coffee differently.

For Pooh's generation, coffee was about staying awake. For millennials, it became about cafés, conversations and lifestyle. Gen Z arrived with questions.

They did not just want a good cup. They wanted context.

Who grew this coffee?

Was the farmer paid fairly?

Did the forest survive this cup?

What happens after I finish drinking it?

Pooh found this shift fascinating. Gen Z did not treat sustainability as a badge or a lecture. For many of them, it was default thinking. If a product harmed people or the planet, it simply felt uncool. Glossy branding impressed them less than transparency.

"Why should I drink something that costs the earth, literally?" a young coffee drinker asked Pooh during a tasting session.

She could not argue with that.

Globally, Gen Z consumers gravitate towards brands that align with their values. Sustainability, ethics, inclusivity and honesty matter. Coffee, being such a personal daily ritual, naturally became part of this value system.

Reusable cups. Plant-based milk. Direct trade beans. Minimal packaging.

These were not trends. They were habits — and coffee brands noticed.

The World Tightens Its Grip

While young consumers reshaped conversations inside cafés, governments were reshaping them outside.

Pooh first encountered the term EUDR, the European Union Deforestation Regulation, while reading an article one evening. She had to read it twice.

The message was blunt: If you want to sell coffee to the EU, prove it did not cause deforestation.

Under the European Union Deforestation Regulation (EUDR), companies placing coffee on the EU market must provide detailed traceability data in the form of satellite data, geo-coordinates and transparent supply chains. These are mandatory requirements; vague assurances no longer suffice.

Europe is one of the most important destinations for Indian coffee exports. This was not just regulation; it was pressure.

In January 2026, India and the European Union announced a landmark trade agreement, described by several commentators as a 'mother of all deals.' The agreement expands access across all 27 EU member states.

The stakes are significant. According to industry export data, nearly 60 per cent of India's green coffee finds its way to Europe.

This opens new possibilities. Indian coffee can move from bulk commodity exports to origin-driven branding. Growers producing distinctive Indian varieties can command better prices and stronger recognition. Exporters can move beyond green beans into roasted, ground and soluble specialty blends. Partnerships with European roasters and specialty cafés are likely to increase visibility for Indian origins.

And Europe is not alone.

Across the world, sustainability requirements are tightening. Climate disclosures, carbon accounting and ethical sourcing audits are becoming standard. What was once optional is now expected.

The message is clear. Coffee can no longer come at the cost of forests, farmers or the future.

Back Home, on Indian Soil

Global regulations may sound sensible in conference rooms, but the reality on Indian coffee farms is far more complex.

Most Indian coffee growers are smallholders who have cultivated coffee for generations. Many farms sit within biodiverse landscapes, alongside pepper, areca nut and fruit trees. Much of Indian coffee, particularly in Karnataka, Kerala and Tamil Nadu, is shade-grown by default.

Ironically, this makes Indian coffee among the most environmentally responsible in the world. Proving it, however, is the challenge.

"How do I provide satellite coordinates when my land was divided by my grandfather?" a grower asked at a discussion Pooh attended.

Documentation, digital mapping and compliance costs are not easy for farmers already dealing with erratic rainfall, rising input costs and labour shortages.

For them, sustainability is not a slogan. It is survival.

Climate change has already altered flowering cycles and yields. Monsoons are unpredictable. Dry spells last longer. Pest outbreaks are more frequent. Coffee farming no longer follows familiar patterns.

Pooh realised something important.

The world was demanding ethical coffee, but the burden of proof was falling squarely on the farmer.

So, What Is the Coffee Board Doing?

This is where the narrative shifts from concern to cautious optimism.

The Coffee Board of India has stepped in to support growers navigating this new environment by organising training programmes on traceability, providing assistance with geo-tagging farms, and advising on meeting international sustainability norms.

There is renewed emphasis on digital records, farmer education and collective compliance models, especially for smallholders who cannot manage these requirements alone.

The Board is also working with exporters, cooperatives and international agencies to ensure Indian coffee does not lose access to global markets simply due to lack of documentation.

India does not need to reinvent sustainable coffee; it just needs to communicate it better.

Long before sustainability became fashionable, Indian coffee farms were growing under forest canopies, supporting biodiversity and relying on traditional knowledge passed down through generations.

Back to the Cup

Pooh finished her coffee and watched the Gen Z girl leave the café, reusable cup in hand.

Something clicked.

A single cup connects a young drinker in Mumbai to a farmer in Coorg, a policymaker in Brussels, a barista in Bandra and a forest that has stood quietly for decades.

Sustainability is not a destination. It is a relationship.

Ethics, at its simplest, is remembering that coffee does not begin at the counter.

As Pooh walked out, she smiled. Coffee had matured. And so had its drinkers.

DID YOU KNOW?

Customisation reigns supreme. According to a report in Coffee Intelligence, 75 per cent of young coffee drinkers opt for flavoured syrups, from classic vanilla to the more extravagant toasted marshmallow.

COMING UP NEXT > Coffee And Youth Identity

CHAPTER 10

COFFEE AND YOUTH IDENTITY

If you want to understand how a city is changing, you don't study its skyline as much as you sit in its cafés. Cities reveal their inner tempo in the small, everyday rituals people return to.

One afternoon, Pooh was seated in a familiar café — not new or fashionable, but the kind where the barista remembers preferences without asking. The tables were full, yet there was no sense of urgency; phones rested beside cups, laptops lay open but unattended, conversations drifted in and out, and although coffee had already been ordered, it was not the main event.

The Cup Before the Sip

Pooh noticed something she had been observing for a while: coffee was being looked at before it was tasted. A young woman adjusted her chair, angled her cup towards the window, waited for the light, and took a photograph carefully framed for Instagram, letting it cool slightly without concern.

People no longer went to cafés only for the beverage. They chose spaces for how they looked and felt, selecting textured walls, lighter tables, and well-lit corners that flattered both cups and faces. The café itself had become part of the experience, even part of the content, to the point where 'Instagrammable cafés' had turned into a widely searched term rather than a passing joke.

Ordering, too, had become more deliberate. Choices around milk, flavour additions, foam, and latte art followed a familiar choreography, and even the act of holding the cup appeared considered, with fingers placed carefully, logos half-visible, and steam caught mid-rise. Coffee was no longer simply consumed; it was presented.

Instagram was not just about display but about presence. In a world where moments passed quickly and attention fractured easily, posting a cup of coffee became a way of saying, *I was here*. This was less about vanity and more about acknowledgement, about marking a moment as worth holding.

Pooh's Survey

Curious about this shift, Pooh informally asked several readers and café regulars some simple questions about their fascination for coffee and also to find out what it costs to set up a cafe in urban India. As she evaluated the responses, a clear pattern emerged. People rarely spoke of coffee as fuel; instead, they described it as comfort, ritual, and something that grounded them during busy days. Flavour mattered, not casually but with care, as did strength, clarity, and aftertaste, all framed in personal terms rather than technical ones.

Aroma appeared repeatedly, especially that first inhale before the sip, carrying with it a sense of reassurance that the cup would justify its price. Pooh noticed how often the idea of trust surfaced quietly in these responses.

Why People Still Visit Cafés

One response stayed with her longer than the rest: "I'm not a regular coffee drinker." And yet, that person still visited cafés. The reason was not caffeine but context.

Cafés were chosen as places where one could sit alone without feeling lonely or meet friends without the pressure of formality. Home coffee was efficient and predictable, while café coffee was intentional, offering permission to linger and exist without explanation. Cafés became modern sanctuaries — not silent or sacred, but safe enough to allow people to simply be.

Watching Orders, Not People

People reveal themselves more through choices than words.

She watched orders being placed.

"Less sugar."

"No sugar."

"Jaggery, if possible."

"Oat milk."

"Just black."

No one made a speech about it. No one justified their choices. They ordered the way they ordered, as if it were obvious.

Coffee had become personal and customised.

She noticed more colour too. Citrus notes. Fruit-infused drinks. Coffee that looked playful — orange brulee cappuccinos, creamy avocado-infused drinks, pale greens and warm browns swirling together. Cups that begged to be photographed, yes — but also tasted lighter, fresher, less punishing.

Global ideas had found their way here quietly, softened by Indian sensibilities. Nothing felt forced. Novelty alone didn't survive long. What stayed was what felt good.

"How Will You Feel Later?"

Coffee conversations had changed as well. Instead of asking only about strength, people now asked whether a drink would upset their stomach, cause a crash later, or feel too sweet. This shift was not driven by restriction but by awareness.

Natural sweeteners appeared without comment, and milk alternatives were no longer special requests. Someone once told Pooh, "I still want to enjoy my coffee. I just don't want it to fight me later," and that sentence stayed with her because it captured how coffee had entered the wellness conversation not as a trend but as a lens through which people evaluated their day.

The Price Question

"Why spend so much on coffee?" was a question that often emerged, usually from those who had not sat long enough in a café to notice what was being exchanged. What people paid for was not just beans or milk but a moment that existed outside obligation.

Price, she realised, was no longer the barrier; perception of value was. Paying ₹250 or more for a cappuccino had been normalised years ago, and people continued to return even with good machines at home because drinking coffee together — or alone among others — carried emotional weight that efficiency could not replace.

Cafés as Places to Become

Pooh has always been drawn to what cafés allow people to become. She had seen freelancers build careers at corner tables, students gain confidence between sips, and casual conversations turn into collaborations. Cafés did not demand purpose; they allowed it to surface naturally.

Menus reflected this shift, expanding beyond food to express philosophy through high-protein options, fibre-conscious plates, and thoughtful indulgences. Consumers had become more informed as well, noticing roast profiles, origins, and brew styles, and judging cafés cup by cup, with bad coffee no longer ignored.

How a City Learns to Pause

Coffee culture is not really about coffee, but about how a city learns to pause. In India, coffee moved from utility to identity, becoming a habit and then a lifestyle, while cafés evolved into spaces designed for lingering, recognition, and shared quiet rather than hurried consumption.

She sensed that the next wave of café culture would emerge not only from metros but from Tier 1 and Tier 2 cities, where aspirational audiences were adopting quickly and both independent cafés and franchises were scaling with confidence.

What the Cup Says

As Pooh finished her coffee and looked around, she felt that people were not redefining coffee to be different but redefining it to be honest. Their choices were not loud declarations but quiet alignments with how they wanted to live, move, and feel.

Coffee had become a daily act of self-expression, something returned to consistently rather than consumed occasionally. If one listened closely, Pooh believed, one could hear a generation finding its voice, one cup at a time.

Instagram-friendly Coffee Trends

Coffee as Atmosphere

Coffee is framed less as a drink and more as a mood. Cups appear beside books, morning light, rumpled bedsheets or open notebooks, turning a simple brew into a curated moment.

Latte Art as Craft

Hearts, rosettes and tulips are no longer fleeting details but part of the performance. Slow pours and close-up shots transform the surface of coffee into something briefly artistic and meant to be shared.

The Café as Backdrop

Décor, natural light and thoughtful design matter as much as the drink itself. Clean lines, textured walls and quiet corners create environments ready to be photographed.

Distinctive Cups and Glassware

The vessel shapes the story. Handcrafted mugs, vintage cups, coconut shells or clear glassware lend personality before the first sip is taken.

Cold Brew and Transparency

Cold brew lends itself naturally to visual storytelling. Transparent cups, visible layers and floating foam allow the drink to be seen as clearly as it is consumed.

Colour and Contrast

Layered lattes and infused drinks — from pistachio to ube — rely on gradients and contrast. Colour becomes part of the appeal, drawing attention before flavour does.

The Beauty of the Process

Preparation is no longer hidden. Stirring, pouring, cracking or whipping become moments worth capturing, reminding viewers that making coffee can be as satisfying as drinking it.

Wellness in Minimal Form

Functional coffees are presented with restraint. Mushroom or collagen blends appear clean and deliberate, where clarity of presentation mirrors clarity of intent.

Short-Form Rituals

Quick videos focus on texture, movement and transformation. In under thirty seconds, a cup moves from ingredients to experience.

Angles and Light

Perspective matters. Slightly overhead shots, natural lighting and vertical framing shape how coffee is perceived long before it is tasted.

COMING UP > Global Coffee Cultures

CHAPTER 11

GLOBAL COFFEE CULTURES

Pooh had long believed that coffee was universal — a simple warmth that could start a morning, anchor a conversation, or gently accompany a quiet pause. A cup seemed like just a cup, beans merely beans, and hot water reliably the same everywhere. But as she travelled — across countries, and sometimes just through books and conversations — she began to notice something deeper. The way people prepared and drank their coffee revealed far more than taste alone. Coffee, she realised, was not simply consumed; it was interpreted. Each culture told its own story through the cup it chose to pour.

Italy

Coffee needs to be precise and purposeful for Italians. Espresso dominates, brewed quickly, consumed standing at the bar, and rarely lingered over. There are rules that go unquestioned: cappuccinos belong to mornings, milk fades out after meals, and espresso punctuates lunch and dinner with quiet regularity. The act is swift and almost transactional, yet deeply embedded in daily life. Italians treat coffee much like conversation — direct, efficient, and intentional — where pleasure lies not in duration but in exactness and coffee energises life without interrupting it.

Turkey

TURKISH COFFEE

Turkish coffee unfolds unhurriedly. Finely ground beans are simmered gently with water in a small pot, with sugar added at the beginning if desired, and the brew is poured unfiltered so the grounds can settle naturally at the bottom of the cup. This is coffee that asks for patience — one that lingers alongside conversation, quiet pauses, and reflection. Even after the last sip, the ritual often continues in the playful reading of fortunes from the patterns left behind. Coffee did not simply end when the cup was empty; it remained, extending the moment and deepening the interaction.

Ethiopia

ETHIOPIAN COFFEE

For families in Ethiopia, coffee drinking is inseparable from community. Beans are roasted over open flames, ground by hand, and brewed in a clay pot, with the aroma announcing the ceremony before the first pour. The process unfolds in stages, shared among guests who sit together, talk, and spend time without hurry. Coffee here is neither fuel nor backdrop; it is the reason people gather.

Japan

Further east, in Japan, coffee moves with quiet precision. Water is poured slowly and deliberately over freshly ground beans, each motion measured, each detail respected — temperature, timing, balance. The process feels almost meditative, as though clarity matters as much as flavour. In Japan, coffee invited stillness. It asked you to slow down, to notice, and to be fully present with the cup in your hands.

Vietnam

VIETNAMESE COFFEE

Vietnamese coffee is strong and distinctive. Dark-roasted beans drip slowly through a metal *phin* filter, often onto sweetened condensed milk. The result — *cà phê sữa đá* — is bold, sweet, and intense, especially when served over ice. Some variations push boundaries further, such as egg coffee, where whipped egg yolk and sugar create a rich foam topping.

France

For the French, coffee belongs to the wider rhythm of leisure. It is rarely rushed and often accompanied by food, conversation, or simple observation. Cafés function as public living rooms where lingering requires no justification. Espresso may be the drink of choice, but the experience extends beyond the cup.

Mexico

In many Mexican homes, coffee is brewed in clay pots with cinnamon and unrefined cane sugar, creating café de olla — aromatic, warming, and deeply domestic. This coffee values continuity over novelty, with spices supporting rather than dominating the flavour. It is meant to comfort and sustain, rooted in familiarity rather than performance.

India

In South India, filter coffee, or kaapi, is prepared using a traditional metal filter that produces a strong decoction, later combined with milk and sugar and poured between vessels to cool and aerate. It is part of daily life, offered instinctively to guests and shared around kitchen tables. Indian filter coffee expresses care more than ceremony, blending routine, hospitality, and familiarity into a single gesture.

North America

North American coffee culture reflects variety and movement. Drip coffee fuels mornings, cold brew stretches into long afternoons, and cafés continually experiment with beans, brewing styles, and milk alternatives. Convenience exists alongside curiosity, allowing people to either repeat familiar choices or seek novelty.

One Bean, Many Expressions

Across cultures, coffee changes form, pace, and meaning, yet its purpose remains consistent. It marks time, creates pauses or momentum, and brings people together, whether briefly or deliberately. As Pooh held her cup, she understood that coffee was never only about waking up; often, it was about recognising how different lives choose to move through their day.

DID YOU KNOW?

What we taste in the cup is only a fraction of coffee's vast story. There are at least 129 species of coffee in the world.

COMING UP > Some Amazing Coffee Stories

CHAPTER 12

SOME AMAZING COFFEE STORIES

By now, Pooh had begun to understand that coffee was never just about taste. Across cultures and centuries, it had repeatedly found itself at the centre of curiosity, controversy, humour, and change. Some stories revealed ingenuity, others excess, and a few bordered on the absurd. Together, they showed how a simple drink acquired layers of meaning far beyond the cup.

Kopi Luwak

Among the most talked-about coffees in the world is Kopi Luwak — a brew that provokes fascination and discomfort in equal measure.

Produced in parts of Indonesia, Kopi Luwak involves the Asian palm civet, a nocturnal mammal that naturally selects the ripest coffee cherries. After consuming the fruit, the civet digests the pulp while the beans pass through intact. These beans are later collected, washed thoroughly, and roasted at high temperatures.

The result is a coffee known for its smoothness and low acidity, often described as earthy or chocolatey. Scarcity and labour-intensive sourcing have driven prices to hundreds of dollars per kilogram.

Yet the story is not without ethical tension. As demand increased, civets were increasingly farmed and confined, raising serious concerns about animal welfare. If rarity created value in Indonesia, reinvention did the same in Switzerland.

Nespresso

Coffee history isn't just shaped by beans and brews — sometimes it's shaped by bold decisions.

When Nespresso first launched, Nestlé believed it would thrive on supermarket shelves. Instead, it quietly failed. Consumers weren't interested in paying a premium for coffee capsules sitting beside instant jars.

Then came a radical shift.

Under CEO Jean-Paul Gaillard, Nespresso was pulled entirely out of supermarkets. Instead of chasing mass appeal, the brand embraced exclusivity. Elegant boutiques replaced grocery aisles. Customers had to register to buy capsules. Coffee wasn't just sold — it was *curated.*

That gamble transformed Nespresso into a global luxury brand and a multibillion-dollar success. Pooh admired the lesson: sometimes, knowing who *not* to sell to is just as important as knowing who to invite in.

Nespresso holds a special place for Pooh. During the pandemic, her son and husband gifted her one. That single gesture lifted her spirits and made staying at home more manageable.

Sweden's Coffee Trial

According to popular accounts, in 18th-century Sweden, coffee was controversial enough to warrant royal scrutiny. King Gustav III, convinced coffee was harmful, ordered an experiment conducted on two identical twins. One was required to drink coffee daily, the other tea. The intent was to observe which beverage led to earlier decline.

The result undermined the hypothesis entirely. Both twins outlived the physicians overseeing the study, and the coffee drinker lived the longest. The experiment quietly ended, leaving coffee's reputation intact.

Vienna's Coffee Houses

In Vienna, cafés evolved into intellectual institutions. Writers, philosophers, and thinkers treated coffee houses as extended workspaces. A single cup justified hours of reading, writing, and debate. Coffee facilitated patience, not speed. The Einspänner — strong coffee topped with cream — was designed to be consumed slowly. Coffee, in this context, was not fuel but framework: a structure around which thought could unfold.

Cafés and the French Revolution

Coffee houses have often doubled as political spaces. In Paris, cafés became gathering points for revolutionary ideas. At the Café de Foy in 1789, Camille Desmoulins delivered a speech that helped ignite popular uprising. Coffee houses offered anonymity, community, and conversation — ingredients as powerful as any weapon. History suggests that ideas often ferment best where people gather casually and think freely.

Turkish Coffee and the Ritual of Interpretation

In Turkey, coffee extends beyond consumption into ritual. After drinking Turkish coffee, the remaining grounds are used for fal — a practice of interpreting patterns to predict the future. Friends gather, speculate, and reflect, knowing the exercise is more symbolic than scientific. The ritual matters less for accuracy than for connection. Coffee becomes an excuse to pause, converse, and imagine together.

Bach's Coffee Cantata

Even classical music acknowledged coffee's hold on society. Johann Sebastian Bach's *Coffee Cantata* humourously depicts a young woman's devotion to coffee, despite her father's objections. Written in the 18th century, it shows that concerns about coffee dependency are far from modern. Cultural anxiety, it seems, has long accompanied caffeine.

The Boston Coffee Shift

After the Boston Tea Party, coffee gained symbolic importance in America. Tea became associated with colonial rule, while coffee emerged as a patriotic alternative. What began as protest gradually evolved into preference, shaping national habits for generations.

Coffee Bans and Resistance

In the Ottoman Empire, coffee was once banned for fear that coffee houses encouraged dissent. Sultan Murad IV imposed harsh punishments, yet coffee consumption persisted underground until the ban eventually collapsed.

Across these stories, coffee appears repeatedly as more than a drink. It functions as social glue, intellectual catalyst, economic experiment, and cultural mirror. It attracts humour, provokes fear, inspires loyalty, and resists control.

Coffee's real strength lay not in caffeine, but in what it enabled — conversation, reflection, rebellion, and ritual — sometimes all at once.

DID YOU KNOW?

Used coffee grounds act as a natural, nutrient-rich fertilizer for plants by providing nitrogen, potassium, phosphorus, and trace minerals like magnesium and copper. When added to soil, they improve structure, enhance water retention, and attract beneficial earthworms.

COMING UP > Cafenomics – Behind the Brew

CHAPTER 13

CAFENOMICS – BEHIND THE BREW

Pooh had not expected the idea of opening a café to be so closely tied to numbers. What began as a creative impulse — good coffee, a welcoming space, meaningful conversations — soon revealed its equally important dimension: capital outlay, margins, monthly burn rates, and the quiet arithmetic that underpins a café's success.

Driven by her larger dream, she approached this with curiosity rather than hesitation. She met café owners across Tier-1 and Tier-2 cities, learning first-hand how they built and sustained their businesses. She connected with equipment manufacturers and wholesalers to understand setup costs, and engaged with manpower consultants to gauge hiring and staffing expenses. This extensive recce of the café ecosystem helped her arrive at a realistic estimate of what it would take to bring her vision to life.

The numbers were significant — but they also told a story of opportunity. According to a report in Mint, India's coffee sector is booming, with exports reaching $1.86 billion in FY26, marking a 20 per cent year-on-year growth. Rising demand for value-added products such as instant coffee and packaged teas is fuelling this expansion, with instant coffee exports alone contributing $498 million between April and January FY26.

Closer home, the steady rise of new cafés and the energy within the ecosystem signalled the same momentum. For Pooh, the numbers were no longer intimidating — they were reassuring. They pointed to a growing market, strong demand, and a business that, when done right, could thrive.

The cafés she admired most made this invisible. Cups arrived unhurried, spaces felt calm and staff moved with confidence. Yet Pooh had learned that this ease was rarely accidental. It was built on planning, restraint and an ongoing negotiation between passion and practicality.

India's café market explains why the stakes are now so high. Industry reports indicate branded café outlets have crossed 5,300 stores nationwide and are expected to exceed 10,000 by 2030.

Urbanisation, remote work, rising disposable incomes and shifting social habits have turned them into hybrid spaces — part office, part meeting room, part social anchor. This has expanded opportunity, but it has also intensified competition. Customers are willing to pay more, but they are also quicker to compare, judge and move on.

When Pooh began asking café owners what it took to open one, the numbers arrived quickly. The breakdown was rarely romantic.

Space

Industry insiders estimate that opening a café in India typically demands an investment ranging anywhere between ₹15 lakh and ₹50 lakh. The spread is wide — and deliberately so — because no two cafés are built on the same ambition.

A 300–400 sq ft neighbourhood café in a Tier-2 city lives by a very different arithmetic than a 1,000 sq ft design-forward space in Mumbai or Bengaluru. In metros, real estate alone can redefine the dream.

Smaller cities offer breathing room. Rents may be half as much, sometimes lower. But reduced costs come with a different challenge — slower walk-ins, longer brand-building cycles and greater patience before profitability. The decision was never simply about cheaper rent. It was about aligning vision with velocity.

Once the lease was secured, the real transformation began. An empty commercial shell rarely resembles a café. Plumbing, electrical systems, exhausts, fire safety compliance and basic infrastructure can together demand ₹5–₹15 lakh. Interiors — lighting, counters, seating, flooring and brand aesthetics — add another ₹5–₹15 lakh for a mid-range café. Premium, design-led spaces can cross ₹20 lakh with ease. Pooh learnt of these numbers when she was researching about cafes and their economics.

Before a single cup is served, the numbers quietly remind the founder of a simple truth: a café may sell comfort, but it is built on capital.

Equipment

A basic professional setup — espresso machine, grinders, refrigeration and kitchen equipment — usually cost ₹2–₹5 lakh, with the espresso machine alone often consuming the largest share. Pooh heard the same lesson repeatedly: good equipment amplifies skill but cannot compensate for poor training. Cheap machines saved money once and lost it slowly through repairs, downtime and inconsistent cups.

Compliance

Licences for food safety, GST, local trade, shop and establishment registration, fire safety and music rights added up to the cost, but missing even one could delay or halt operations entirely. It was a small cost with disproportionate consequences.

Inventory

Coffee beans, milk, food items, syrups, takeaway packaging and cleaning supplies required an initial outlay of ₹50,000 to ₹1.5 lakh, and constant replenishment thereafter. Tracking wastage, portion control and milk loss becomes extremely important. Those who planned credit terms with vendors and engineered menus carefully survived longer.

Technology

Point-of-Sale (POS) systems, billing software and inventory management tools add to the cost but also reduce errors and reveal sales patterns. Pooh noticed that cafés without this visibility often relied on instinct until losses became undeniable.

Marketing

Even the best cafés struggled if they opened quietly. Branding, signage, launch campaigns and social media visibility typically required ₹50,000 to ₹1 lakh or more initially, followed by steady monthly spends. In a market saturated with options, being good was not enough; being remembered mattered.

Operating Costs

Operating costs like salaries, utilities, maintenance, raw materials and delivery platform commissions could easily add to the cost. On paper, well-managed cafés could achieve profit margins of 10–20 per cent. In practice, those margins belonged only to operators who secured repeat customers, controlled waste meticulously and approached breakeven timelines with patience rather than optimism.

In the end, margins were managed in spreadsheets. But reputation was built in human interaction.

As Pooh sat in a familiar café, watching orders placed without explanation — oat milk, jaggery, black — she realised that successful cafés were not chasing flash. They were chasing clear audiences, focused menus, controlled costs, and systems that worked quietly in the background.

Opening a café in India, she concluded, was neither an indulgence nor a shortcut to profit. It was a business built on repetition, discipline and patience, where creativity mattered, but spreadsheets mattered just as much. Coffee might invite the first visit, but consistency decided whether people came back.

Sometimes, a good coffee experience isn't really about coffee at all. It's about how carefully everything else has been thought through.

DID YOU KNOW?

The coffee sector sustains the livelihoods of over two million people, who are engaged in cultivation, processing, and trade.

COMING UP > What is Coming Next?

CHAPTER 14

WHAT IS COMING NEXT?

The story of coffee is often explained through waves. It is a useful shorthand for understanding how tastes evolve, how industries mature, and how values shift over time. Yet what lies ahead feels less like another wave breaking and more like a widening field of concerns.

To see where coffee is going, it helps to briefly revisit how it arrived here.

A Brief Look Back

The First Wave was about access. Coffee became mass-produced, shelf-stable and easy to prepare. Instant coffee entered homes and offices. Convenience mattered more than flavour. Coffee functioned as reliable fuel.

The Second Wave brought coffee into public life. Coffee houses emerged as spaces to meet and linger. Espresso drinks, flavoured syrups and café culture took hold. Experience became as important as the beverage itself.

The Third Wave reframed coffee as craft. Single-origin beans, traceability, brewing methods and flavour notes moved to the forefront. Farmers were named. Roasters told stories. Baristas were recognised as skilled professionals. Coffee was treated less like a commodity and more like an expressive agricultural product.

Each wave layered itself over the previous one. Accessibility did not disappear when craft emerged. Experience did not vanish when origin took centre stage. Coffee evolved by accumulation, not replacement.

And now, gradually, a Fourth Wave has taken shape.

Defining the Fourth Wave

If earlier waves were shaped by what and how we drink, this one is shaped by why.

The Fourth Wave widens the lens. It considers not only the cup, but the system behind it — soil health, farmer livelihoods, supply chains, technology and consumer awareness.

At its heart are three interconnected shifts.

First, sustainability has moved from marketing language to operational necessity. Ethical sourcing, environmental responsibility and long-term viability are no longer peripheral concerns. Questions about labour conditions, climate impact and pricing transparency now sit at the centre of serious coffee conversations.

Second, technology has quietly moved from novelty to foundation. Precision brewers, roast-profiling software and data-guided quality checks now sit seamlessly within daily practice, supporting consistency and transparency. It no longer stands apart from craft — it works alongside it. What was once occasional brilliance becomes dependable excellence.

Data gently informs roasting curves and inventory decisions, while smart brewing devices steady variables that once relied entirely on intuition. Skill is not replaced — it is steadied, extended and shared.

Online communities carry this learning further. A technique refined in one city travels easily to another, crossing borders without ceremony.

Rather than creating distance, technology has opened the conversation wider, inviting more people to understand, question and participate in the cup before them.

Third, connection has deepened across the chain. Roasters build long-term partnerships with farmers. Direct trade models create dialogue instead of distance. Cafés increasingly educate customers through tastings, workshops and everyday conversation. The gap between professional and consumer narrows.

Alongside these shifts is a rise in flavour literacy. Coffee drinkers are more curious about origin, processing methods and seasonal variation. Menus read less like price lists and more like guides. Drinking coffee becomes an act of attention.

In this environment, coffee is not simply purchased. It is understood.

Today, and Beyond

The Fourth Wave represents a shift in perception as much as practice. Coffee is evaluated not only by taste or presentation, but by impact — environmental, social and cultural.

For emerging brands and independent cafés, this shift brings both opportunity and responsibility. Participation requires more than adopting tools. It demands better questions.

Will there be a Fifth Wave? Perhaps. But progress may not arrive as a clean break. Earlier priorities — accessibility, craft, experience — continue to matter. What lies ahead may be less about declaring a new era and more about integration: affordability aligned with ethics, craft strengthened by technology, growth balanced with responsibility.

Home is where it all began

The kettle clicked off. Pooh reached automatically for two tins — tea for her dear hubby, coffee for herself and her *beta*. Some rituals had quietly settled into permanence.

"For someone who has written a book about coffee," her husband said, watching her measure the leaves, "you are remarkably loyal to my tea."

"I respect loyalty," she replied.

Over the years he had accompanied her to countless cafés — listening patiently as she spoke to baristas about origins and processing, waiting while she photographed cups, nodding through flavour notes he could not quite taste. He ordered tea every time. Sometimes reluctantly from short menus. But he went because she loved it.

He did not drink coffee. But he always showed up for it.

At the counter the coffee bloomed. Her son leaned closer.

"New roast?"

"Experimental," she said. "Different processing."

They carried their cups to the table. Two deep mugs. One porcelain teacup.

Her son took the first sip. "It's bright… but it changes as you drink it."

"That's the point," Pooh smiled. "It unfolds."

Her husband watched them with quiet amusement. "You both speak about it like it's alive."

"In a way it is," she said. "Soil. Weather. Hands. Time."

"And where does it go from here?" he asked.

Her son thought for a moment. "More transparent. More thoughtful. Maybe kinder to the people who grow it."

There was a small pause. He looked at their cups, then at his own.

"There must be one coffee in this world I could try," he said, almost to himself.

Pooh did not rush the moment.

"We'll find your cup," she said.

Outside, the evening was settling over the city. Somewhere shutters were lowering. Somewhere a roaster was finishing the day's batch. Far away, farmers were tending land that would shape harvests none of them could yet taste.

Inside, steam rose gently between leaf and bean.

He lifted his teacup.

"To your movement."

Pooh raised her mug. Her son followed.

"To curiosity," she said softly.

For a while they simply sat there.

The cups grew lighter. The conversation slowed. The quiet between them felt complete.

Coffee had travelled through centuries and continents to arrive at tables like this one. Through farmers and traders, roasters and baristas, through invention, curiosity and care.

Yet in the end, it returned to something very simple.

A kettle, the three cups, and the people who gather around them.

The waves would come — they always do.

But tonight, the story rested here.

And somewhere, perhaps, another cup was already waiting to be discovered.

COMING UP > Coffee Glossary

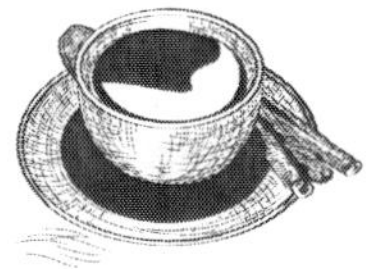

CHAPTER 15
COFFEE GLOSSARY

This comprehensive coffee glossary introduces key terms from bean to brew, helping readers navigate the language of coffee with confidence.

COFFEE SPECIES AND BEAN TYPES

Arabica (*Coffea arabica*) – The most widely consumed coffee species, prized for its nuanced flavours, higher acidity, and aromatic complexity.

Robusta (*Coffea canephora*) – A hardier species with higher caffeine content, stronger bitterness, and heavier body, commonly used in espresso blends.

Liberica (*Coffea liberica*) – A rare coffee species with large beans and a distinctive smoky, floral, and fruity profile.

Excelsa (*Coffea liberica var. dewevrei*) – A Liberica variant known for tart, dark, fruity notes, often used to add depth to blends.

COFFEE CULTIVARS AND BEAN VARIATIONS

Bourbon – A classic Arabica cultivar valued for sweetness and balance.

Caturra – A natural mutation of Bourbon, known for productivity and quality.

Geisha (also known as Gesha) – A highly prized, aromatic Arabica cultivar with tea-like and floral characteristics.

Kona – Coffee grown in Hawaii's Kona region, typically smooth and mild.

Maragogipe – Large-sized Arabica beans, often called "elephant beans."

Peaberry – A natural mutation where only one round bean forms inside the cherry.

Typica – One of the oldest and most foundational Arabica cultivars.

ROAST LEVELS AND ROASTING CONCEPTS

Roasting – The heating process that transforms green beans into aromatic, flavourful coffee.

Roasting Degree – Indicates how light or dark beans are roasted, from light development after first crack to very dark roasts.

Roast Profile – The specific heat and airflow pattern used during roasting.

Roast Date – The date beans were roasted, used as an indicator of freshness.

Light Roast – Preserves origin flavours with higher acidity and floral or fruity notes.

Medium Roast – Offers balance between acidity, body, and roast character.

Dark Roast – Produces smoky, bold flavours with reduced acidity and visible surface oils.

COFFEE PROCESSING METHODS (POST-HARVEST)

Natural / Dry Process – Cherries are dried whole, producing sweet, fruity, wine-like flavours.

Washed / Wet Process – Fruit is removed before drying, resulting in cleaner, brighter cups.

Honey Process – Pulp is partially left on the bean, balancing sweetness and acidity.

HARVESTING AND FARMING PRACTICES

Hand Picking – Selective harvesting of ripe cherries to ensure quality.

Strip Picking – Removing all cherries at once, resulting in mixed ripeness and lower quality.

Current Crop – Coffee harvested in the current season, valued for freshness.

Old Crop – Coffee from the previous harvest, typically less vibrant in flavour.

Seasonal Coffee – Limited-availability coffee tied to specific harvest periods.

Micro-lot – Small, high-quality lots from a single farm or section.

Single Origin – Coffee sourced from one country, region, or estate.

COFFEE BEVERAGES (ESPRESSO-BASED AND OTHERS)

Espresso – A concentrated coffee brewed under pressure, forming the base of many drinks.

Americano – Espresso diluted with hot water for a lighter body.

Cappuccino – Espresso topped with steamed milk and a thick foam layer.

Latte – Espresso with a generous amount of steamed milk.

Flat White – Espresso with velvety microfoam and minimal froth.

Macchiato – Espresso lightly 'stained' with a small amount of milk.

Cortado – Espresso 'cut' with equal or near-equal milk.

Lungo – Espresso extracted longer with more water.

Ristretto – A shorter, more concentrated espresso shot.

Mocha – Espresso combined with chocolate and milk.

Affogato – Espresso poured over a scoop of ice cream.

Filter Coffee – Brewed coffee without pressure, producing a larger, lighter cup.

Cold Brew Coffee – Coffee extracted slowly using cold water.

Cold Drip Coffee (Kyoto-style) – Cold water dripped over grounds for extended extraction.

BREWING METHODS AND EXTRACTION TECHNIQUES

Pour-over Coffee – Manual brewing by steadily pouring water over coffee grounds.

Immersion – Grounds are fully immersed in water during extraction.

Extraction – The process of dissolving flavours from coffee into water.

Bloom – Initial wetting of grounds to release trapped gases.

Brewing Ratio – The proportion of coffee grounds to water.

Brewing Temperature – Water heat level affecting flavour extraction.

Brewing Time – Duration water contacts the coffee grounds.

COFFEE BREWING EQUIPMENT AND TOOLS

Chemex – A pour-over brewer producing clean, aromatic coffee.

French Press – An immersion brewer using a metal plunger.

Moka Pot – A stovetop brewer using steam pressure.

Syphon – A vacuum-based brewing device.

V60 – A cone-shaped pour-over dripper with spiral ridges.

Portafilter – The handled basket holding espresso grounds.

Tamper – Tool used to compress coffee grounds evenly.

GRINDING AND PREPARATION

Grind Size – The coarseness or fineness of ground coffee.

Puck – The compressed disk of used espresso grounds.

SENSORY ATTRIBUTES, FLAVOURS, AND MOUTHFEEL

Aroma – The smell of coffee, comprising hundreds of aromatic compounds.

Body – The tactile weight or texture of coffee in the mouth.

Bitterness – A sharp flavour often associated with dark roasts or over-extraction.

Bright – A lively, acidic sensation on the palate.

Briny – A salty or mineral-like note, sometimes linked to water chemistry or processing factors.

Earthy – Flavours reminiscent of soil or damp forest floor.

Crema – The foam layer atop a well-pulled espresso.

COFFEE CHEMISTRY AND COMPOUNDS

Caffeine – The stimulant responsible for coffee's energising effect.

Trigonelline – A compound contributing to aroma and diuretic properties.

COFFEE TASTING, EVALUATION, AND QUALITY SYSTEMS

Cupping – A professional tasting method to evaluate coffee quality.

Q Grading – A certification system that trains and licenses professionals to evaluate coffee quality using standardised scoring protocols.

Cup of Excellence (COE) – A prestigious competition recognising top coffees.

Specialty Coffee – Coffee scoring 80 points or higher on the Specialty Coffee Association (SCA) 100-point scale.

COFFEE PROFESSIONALS AND CAFÉ CULTURE

Barista – A trained professional who prepares and serves coffee beverages.

Latte Art – Decorative patterns created with steamed milk.

ETHICAL, TRADE, AND CERTIFICATION TERMS

Fairtrade – A certification system designed to ensure minimum pricing and improved trading conditions for coffee farmers.

COFFEE PLANT, BIOLOGY, AND PESTS

Bean – The seed of the coffee cherry.

Cherry – The fruit containing the coffee bean.

Green Coffee Beans – Unroasted coffee beans.

Coffee Berry Borer – A destructive beetle that burrows into coffee cherries and damages the seed.

Coffee Leaf Rust – A fungal disease (*Hemileia vastatrix*) that reduces yield and threatens global production.

MAJOR COFFEE-PRODUCING COUNTRIES (BY VOLUME)

Brazil

The world's largest coffee producer, contributing a significant share of global output, primarily Arabica. Brazil plays a significant role in influencing global volume and pricing.

Vietnam

The second-largest producer globally, known for its dominance in Robusta beans, widely used in instant coffee and espresso blends.

Colombia

Renowned for high-quality, mild Arabica coffee, often associated with balance, consistency, and clean flavour profiles.

Indonesia

Produces distinctive coffees from its many islands, with regions like Sumatra known for earthy, complex, and full-bodied beans.

Ethiopia

Considered the birthplace of Arabica coffee, offering exceptional diversity in flavour, processing styles, and genetic varieties.

Other Major Producers

Honduras, India, Uganda, Peru, and Mexico — important contributors to global supply, often shaping blends and regional consumption patterns.

KEY COFFEE-GROWING REGIONS

The Coffee Belt

A tropical zone between the Tropic of Cancer and the Tropic of Capricorn where coffee can be grown commercially.

Primary Production Zones

South America, Southeast Asia, and Africa — regions where climate, altitude, and tradition combine to support large-scale coffee cultivation.

COMING UP > Sources & References

SOURCES & REFERENCES

This book draws upon journalistic articles, institutional reports, industry publications, and brand archives that informed its broader context and research. While the interpretations and narrative voice remain the author's own, the following sources were consulted during the writing process.

Alpen Sierra Coffee. n.d. "Sustainable and Ethical Sourcing of Coffee – A Guide to Responsible Practices." *Alpen Sierra Coffee.* https://alpensierracoffee.com/blog-article/sustainable-ethical-sourcing-coffee/

Begum, Balqees. 2020. "Dalgona Coffee: A Quarantine Drink That Has Become My Ritual." *Medium.* https://medium.com/@balqeesbegum512/dalgona-coffee-a-quarantine-drink-that-has-become-my-ritual-968df40acb1c

Khanna, Sundeep. 2022. "Backstory in India: The Cups That Cheers Is Always Bru or Nescafé." *CNBC-TV18.* https://www.cnbctv18.com/business/companies/backstory-in-india-the-cups-that-cheers-is-always-bru-or-nescafe-13120162.htm

Coffee Board of India. 2026. "Coffee Statistical Report." *Coffee Board of India.*

Coffee Bros. 2023. "Specialty Coffee Glossary." *Coffee Bros.* https://coffeebros.com/blogs/coffee/specialty-coffee-glossary

Manchanada, Kunal. 2025. "Blue Tokai Posts Rs 325 Cr Revenue in FY25, Cuts Losses by 21%." *Entrackr.* https://entrackr.com/fintrackr/blue-tokai-posts-rs-325-cr-revenue-in-fy25-cuts-losses-by-21-10918097

Essense Coffee. 2019. "The Ultimate Coffee Glossary." *Essense Coffee.* https://essense.coffee/en/the-ultimate-coffee-glossary/

Ravidas, Preetika. 2025. "What's Driving the Rise of Hojicha, Climate Cafés, and Culture." *Firstpost.* https://www.firstpost.com/lifestyle/whats-driving-the-rise-of-hojicha-climate-cafes-and-culture-13956909.html

Sarkar, Suhel. 2025. "How India Acquired a Taste for Specialty Coffee." *Fresh Cup Magazine.* https://freshcup.com/how-india-acquired-a-taste-for-specialty-coffee/

Halmaritea. 2025. "Why Indians Prefer Tea Over Coffee: A Cultural Insight." *Halmaritea.* https://www.halmaritea.com/blog/why-indians-prefer-tea-over-coffee/

Roman, Ivan. 2025. "6 Ways Coffee Helped Transform the World." *History.com.* https://www.history.com/articles/coffee-history-facts

Indian Coffee House. n.d. "Official Website." *Indian Coffee House.*

International Coffee Organization. 2026. "Coffee Market Report." *International Coffee Organization.*

Kodagu Express. 2026. "India-EU Free Trade Deal Set to Boost Coffee Exports, Says Coffee Board." *Kodagu Express.* https://

www.kodaguexpress.com/post/india-eu-free-trade-deal-set-to-boost-coffee-exports-says-coffee-board

Perfect Daily Grind. 2020. "Exploring the Dalgona Coffee Craze." *Perfect Daily Grind.* https://perfectdailygrind.com/2020/04/exploring-the-dalgona-coffee-craze/

Perfect Daily Grind. 2025. "Specialty Coffee Is Expanding in India – and the Market Shows Promise." *Perfect Daily Grind.* https://perfectdailygrind.com/2025/05/specialty-coffee-india-international-roasters/

Press Information Bureau, Government of India. 2025. "Brewing Prosperity: India's Coffee Story from Farm to Global Fame." *Press Information Bureau.* https://www.pib.gov.in/PressReleasePage.aspx?PRID=2196210

Arora, Ridvika. 2025. "Cost of Opening a Cafe in India: Complete Investment Breakdown." *RestroWorks.* https://www.restroworks.com/blog/cost-of-opening-a-cafe-in-india/

Sacred Grounds Coffee Roasters. 2025. "The Fourth Wave of Coffee: A New Era of Coffee Culture." *Sacred Grounds Coffee Roasters.* https://www.sacredgrounds.coffee/single-post/the-fourth-wave-of-coffee-a-new-era-of-coffee-culture

Rao, Rukmini, and Prosenjit Dutta. 2025. "A New Book Charts How Café Coffee Day Catered to the Youth and the Fashionable Set." *Scroll.in.* https://scroll.in/article/1088520/a-new-book-charts-how-cafe-coffee-day-catered-to-the-youth-as-well-as-the-fashionable-set

SIG Group. 2024. "Transforming Coffee Culture in India: A Sustainable Packaging Revolution." *SIG Group*. https://www.sig.biz/en-in/news-insights/blog/transforming-coffee-culture-in-india-a-sustainable-packaging-revolution

Young Urban Project. 2025. "Starbucks International Strategy – A Case Study for Global Success." *Young Urban Project*. https://www.thestrategyinstitute.org/insights/starbucks-international-strategy-a-case-study-for-global-success

Harsh Kumar. "India's Coffee, Tea Exports Rise on Value-Added Products, Global Demand." Mint, 2026. https://www.livemint.com/industry/india-coffee-tea-exports-value-added-products-global-demand-records-11774505484014.html

STAY CONNECTED

The journey of coffee does not end with this book.

Through her popular Instagram handle *Coffee Tales with Pooh*, Purvi continues to explore cafés, brewing techniques, sustainability conversations, and the evolving culture of coffee — one cup at a time.

If this book resonated with you, you are warmly invited to join the ongoing conversation.

Follow:

Instagram – @coffeetalesbypooh

Because the Caffeine Movement is still unfolding.